"As a SCORE Counselor for small businesses, Executive Coach with an international HR consulting firm, and in my private practice, I have used *The Secret Side of Anger* with some of my clients. I shared Janet's concepts with one of my senior executive clients for a Fortune 100 company, suffering from temper and rage incidents. I was able to provide him with coping techniques and behavior modification changes which has allowed him to successfully control his anger and be a more effective executive. As for myself, I am a changed person as a result of listening to her audio book. Thank you, Janet, for your down-to-earth guidance!"

-Bill Baldwin, Owner of EMD Group, LLC

THE
SECRET SIDE
OF ANGER

THE
SECRET SIDE
OF ANGER

The Quickest & Easiest
Guide (Ever!) to
Managing Anger

JANET PFEIFFER

TATE PUBLISHING *& Enterprises*

This book is designed to provide accurate and authoritative information with regard to the subject matter covered. This information is given with the understanding that neither the author nor Tate Publishing, LLC is engaged in rendering legal, professional advice. Since the details of your situation are fact dependent, you should additionally seek the services of a competent professional.

The opinions expressed by the author are not necessarily those of Tate Publishing, LLC.

Published by Tate Publishing & Enterprises, LLC
127 E. Trade Center Terrace | Mustang, Oklahoma 73064 USA
1.888.361.9473 | www.tatepublishing.com

Tate Publishing is committed to excellence in the publishing industry. The company reflects the philosophy established by the founders, based on Psalm 68:11,
"The Lord gave the word and great was the company of those who published it."

Book design copyright © 2009 by Tate Publishing, LLC. All rights reserved.
Cover design by Tate Publishing
Interior design by Nathan Harmony

Published in the United States of America

ISBN: 978-1-60696-530-6
1. Self-Help: Anger Management
2. Self-Help: Personal Growth: General
09.03.05

DEDICATION

First and always, I want to thank my Creator for all of the many blessings and gifts he has go graciously bestowed on me and for entrusting me with the responsibility of delivering his message of peace to others. I am truly honored and humbled by this great privilege.

Secondly, to my two wonderful therapists, who are responsible for my being alive today, Mary McGinnity and Eleanor Buscher. Without your guidance, knowledge, encouragement, and support, I would not have survived the most dangerous period of my life. I owe my life to both of you. You are my angels.

To my children, who suffered needlessly due to my own ignorance and personal issues and have chosen to forgive me for the suffering I caused them. I am eternally grateful to have you in my life and inspired by your tremendous capacity to love.

To my mother, who has been my greatest role model in teaching me the ways to inner peace, and to my dad for always being proud and supportive of me. I love you both.

TABLE OF CONTENTS

INTRODUCTION

I'm a really nice person. Ask anyone who knows me. They'll tell you that I am one of the kindest people you'll ever meet. Ask anyone, that is, except for the ones I've hurt. They'll paint a very different picture of me, and rightfully so.

I am a good person, but like most of us, I knew virtually nothing about anger. When I was a child, I was basically allowed to express two emotions: happy and happy. Negative feelings were considered unacceptable and inappropriate. I learned early on in life that no one wanted do deal with someone who was upset, sad, angry, depressed, or hurting. Maybe it's because people are inadequately prepared to handle it and feel uncomfortable themselves. I don't know.

What I do know for certain is that for the first portion of my life, I kept my negative feelings to myself. I tucked away the deep-rooted pain and my irrational (but very real to me) fears. I suppressed my feelings of loneliness and low self-esteem. I believed that if I denied them they would go away; if I ignored them, then they didn't really exist. Nothing could have been further from the truth. This practice would later send me into a downward spiral of self-destructive behavior.

Throughout my teenage years, I suffered from depression and anxiety attacks. Never revealing the truth to anyone, I kept those feelings to myself as well, believing that no one really cared, nor was anyone interested in what I had to say.

As a young mother in my twenties, I found myself trapped in a painful marriage with a man who did not want to be with me. The stress of trying to project the image of being the perfect all-American family was a charade that became impossible to maintain. Once again, loneliness, sadness, hurt, frustration, and anger festered inside me until I could no longer contain it. Like an erupting volcano, I spewed my anger onto the innocent bystanders I called my children. Years of pent-up emotions boiled over and scorched the bodies and hearts of the ones I loved most, leaving behind lifelong scars.

A shroud of guilt and shame became an additional burden for me to bear, haunting my daily existence. I couldn't find my way out of my self-imposed hell.

My behavior fluctuated from suppressing my anger to lashing out to self-destructive behaviors (such as bulimia and abusive relationships) to self-loathing and even thoughts of dying. Depression resurfaced, and fear emotionally paralyzed me.

Through the grace of God and two incredible therapists, I began to learn about my anger. I discovered the real reasons why there was so much rage inside me. I discovered that it wasn't about the anger at all. I learned to identify the underlying—or root—emotions and heal them. I learned how to resolve the internal issues that were responsible for my distress and experienced far less anger than ever before.

I realized that no one could hurt my feelings or make me angry—that it was my choice. I learned that I had power over my own life and happiness.

I developed an insatiable appetite for acquiring knowledge about anger. It fascinated me, and I read every book I could find. I spoke to every professional I knew. This was the key that was unlocking doors for me. Finally, there was hope. I examined my own life. I developed skills that I could use to express, manage, and reduce my own anger.

I began to heal the pain and replace the rage with understanding that ultimately led to inner peace and serenity. And when I did, my entire life was transformed. It wasn't easy, but it was definitely worth the time and energy. Miracles do happen, and the amazing thing is that it is within our power to create them.

I have devoted the past fifteen years of my life to sharing my knowledge, expertise, life experience, and skills with thousands of others in the workshops and seminars I present throughout the country. My hope is that I can provide for them the tools to make their lives safer, happier, more loving, and joyful; to teach them where their personal power lies and how to use it; to help them understand that they are not powerless victims being manipulated by others or by their circumstances. My focus is to teach others how to create lasting peace within themselves as I and thousands of others have. And the beauty of it all is that it is not hard to do.

Nobody deserves to hurt or be hurt. We can create peace and harmony within our lives, but only if we have the proper knowledge and the necessary skills to do so. This book contains both.

Some believe that when you have your health, you have it all. I believe that when you have inner peace, you have everything.

My mission in life is to share with others the mistakes I've made and the lessons I've learned so they can avoid the same kind of suffering I've endured and causing the same kind of pain I've caused others. It is my sincere desire to assist them in creating abundant joy, happiness, and lasting peace in their lives.

In the words of St. Francis, "Lord, make me an instrument of your peace."

God bless.

INQUIRING MINDS NEED TO KNOW

Have you ever been angry?
Of course you have!

Do you know where that anger *really* comes from?
Probably not.

Do you always manage and express your anger appropriately?
I didn't think so.

Do you blow up when you get mad?
Yikes!

Or do you try to control it and keep it inside?
Not good either.

How well do you deal with someone else who's angry?
That badly, huh?

Would you like to gain new insights and a deeper understanding of anger?
Of course you would!

Would you like innovative tools for managing it effectively?
I knew it!

Would you like to learn how to prevent others from pushing your buttons and getting you angry in the first place?
Well, yeah! Who wouldn't?

Then you have come to the right place! So let's get started!

PART 1

GET SMART

THE ANGER DIET

HOW TO REDUCE
AND REGAIN

Let me first congratulate you on your commitment to learning about this misunderstood emotion. You obviously want to improve the quality of your life and the lives of those around you. I applaud you for that. (Can you hear me clapping?)

Too often, people fail to recognize the need to change how they behave when it comes to being angry. Even fewer are willing to work on making the necessary changes. I can't tell you (well, actually I could tell you if I wanted to) how many times I hear people use the lame excuse that, "This is just the way I am. Deal with it." Wrong! It's the way they *choose* to be. Life is about choices, and anger is one of them.

True, most of us were never taught appropriate methods

of expressing, managing, and responding to anger. But as adults, it becomes our responsibility to reexamine our beliefs and behaviors from time to time to see if what we are doing needs to change. We need to make sure that how we are treating ourselves and others is the best it can be. Too often, we become complacent in our behavior and refuse to grow. We offer lame excuses: "I can't help it," "He makes me mad," "It's not my fault." Ooh! That really gets my goat. (Well, I don't actually have a goat, but if I did...)

Behavior is learned. Someone, somewhere in your life, taught you how to express your anger. But not everything we learned as children was accurate and valid. There are few people in this world who were ever trained in anger management. Some may have developed mediocre strategies that are hit and miss (I mean that *figuratively*: hitting is not good, so please don't do it) and passed them on to us. A few may have even gotten really good at "controlling" their anger (although trying to control anger is like putting a Tupperware lid on a volcano to keep it from erupting...it's not very effective). And yes, there are some who have definitely mastered the art of keeping the peace. If you are reading this book, you probably do not fall into the latter category.

But not to worry—you have *me*! (Oh come on, I'm not that bad. Just give me a chance.) I am going to teach you things about anger that you never knew before: things that will dramatically improve the quality of your life and the lives of those around you. You will learn how to express yourself without offending others. You will discover the most effective way of responding to someone who's angry.

I'll show you what lies beneath the anger and how to

identify the root cause, not just what's triggering it. You will learn to assert yourself in ways that gain cooperation and respect from others. Using a simple three-step process, you will break the explosive/aggressive cycle of behavior that is so detrimental to your health and relationships. I will even show you how to prevent others from pushing your buttons and getting you angry in the first place. Doesn't that sound wonderful? Of course it does.

It's not hard. It's just that no one ever taught you before. I'm going to change that for you. In fact, I'm going to put you on a strict anger diet (oh, yeah, just what the world needs, another diet). Yes, as a matter of fact, it most definitely does need *this* diet.

> In as little as twenty minutes a day, you will:
> *Shed* those unwanted outbursts of rage,
> *Eliminate* unsightly frustration,
> *Shape* and *tone* your way to a more serene
> and confident you.

> You will get "FIT with Pfeiffer" and
> *Reduce* the Frequency of your anger
> *Reduce* the Intensity of your anger
> *Reduce* the amount of Time you spend being angry.

> And as an added bonus,
> you will *regain* inner peace, happiness, and harmony.
> So, sit back and get comfortable because your life is
> about to change *forever*!

WHAT'S IN
A WORD?

Before we begin discussing anger, it's important to have a clear definition of what we're speaking about. That's why I like to consult with the experts (oh, wait, that's *me*). Even so, I got a second opinion from the original expert, Webster. The universal meaning of anger is: "a feeling of displeasure or distress caused by feelings of powerlessness or helplessness." Remember those two words, *powerless* and *helpless*. We'll refer to them periodically throughout this book.

I have a very simple and completely accurate definition of my own. Anger, very simply stated, is a sign that there are unmet needs and expectations. Think about it. As long as I have what I need, I'm reasonably content and generally easy to get along with. When things don't go my way (unmet needs or expectations), I become agitated, annoyed, maybe even hostile.

How many of you have babies? (I see a lot of hands going

up.) For those of you who don't, can you remember when you were a baby? (Me neither. It's been too many years.) When an infant is hungry, she cries. It's her way of letting you know that she needs to be fed. As long as you satisfy her need, the anger dissipates, and you have a happy little bundle of joy. (Unless, of course, she has gas and needs to be burped...or worse: a dirty diaper. Yuck!) But you get my point. Babies have needs. It may be the need to be held and cuddled, the need to sleep, the need to feel safe. When we provide children with their basic needs, they are content. This, however, can present quite a challenge since babies can't usually talk and let us know exactly what they want from us. So, we have to keep our fingers crossed as we journey through the process of elimination.

We're no different from babies (except that we're a lot larger and we have more hair; well, *some* have more hair, not all—not my husband). We go through life continually having needs that must be satisfied. The primary difference here is that as adults it becomes our responsibility to be able to iden-tify and fulfill our own needs. And that's not always easy.

How many of us go through life oblivious to our own desires? We're so busy taking care of our daily obligations that we run on autopilot. We focus more on what's going on around us and pay very little attention to what is going on inside of us. Unidentified needs arise, go unnoticed and unattended, and suddenly we react to a situation without a deep understanding of what just happened or why. *Awareness is key*. We need to start paying attention to our inner selves. Spending time alone getting to know yourself is critical to being able to reduce the amount of anger you experience. Let's take a closer look at this.

Have you ever found yourself in this situation? You're late for work. You fly out of the house with donut in hand and race down the highway. Or so you had hoped. You soon come to realize that every other driver in the state decided to take the exact same route at the precise same hour of the morning. And now you're sitting in bumper-to-bumper traffic. (You *do* know that all of those other drivers did this on purpose just to annoy you?) "Son of a _____! Don't you people know that I'm late for work?" you shout. Even if they could hear you, would it really matter? Everyone here is in the same predicament.

Where do needs and expectations come into play in this situation? If I expect that the roads will be relatively free of traffic during rush hour (isn't it interesting that it's called "rush hour" when we're all actually *stuck* in traffic and not rushing at all?), is what I'm anticipating fair and reasonable? Probably not. But if that's what I believe will take place and it doesn't, I'm going to be disappointed and very likely angry. A readjustment in expectations to what is more realistic will alleviate my frustration. If I expect traffic, I can prepare myself for it ahead of time. I may not be happy about it, but at least I knew what was coming.

And needs: if you don't know what you need, how will you know how to get it? Satisfying the basic need is an important part of reducing anger. So, what is the obvious need here? There are two things I want you to keep in mind: the need must be specific, and it must be *reasonable*. To answer, "I need for everyone to get off the road so I can get to work" is way out of line with reality. Your expectations are unreasonable. It's never going to happen. The real need here is for you, the driver, to be able to get to work on time. Is that a fair request? Maybe yes, maybe no. It depends on a lot of different factors.

If what I'm looking for is within reason, then I need to shift my focus off of what the problem is (I'm late for work) and on to the solution. I have to go to plan B. (*Always* have a plan B. Life rarely goes according to our original plans.) I need to get to work on time. Is this the only route I can take? Are there any other roads that might be less congested where I can make better time? If so, then let me take that route as soon as possible. It might also be a good idea at this time to give your boss a call and let him know your situation. Although he may still be annoyed, giving someone a heads-up can sometimes lessen the consequences.

At the very least, it shows that you are a responsible and considerate employee. You might also want to think about stopping at Dunkin Donuts to pick up his favorite. A little token of remorse (aka bribery) can't hurt. Then own up to the inconvenience you caused him, offer an apology, make amends (you might want to work through lunch to make up for lost time), and learn from your mistake. Vow to handle things better in the future, perhaps leaving more time for your commute.

If I have a plan, I am not powerless. (Remember that word?) I take responsibility, make alternative choices, and have some control over the outcome of this situation. That gives me a sense of power and confidence and eases my angst.

On the other hand, if what I'm requesting is unrealistic, at that time, in this place, under these circumstances, with those who are present, and with all the conditions being imposed, then I need to reevaluate the situation. Can I accept my current set of circumstances and make the best out of it? There are many conditions we find ourselves in in life that we have no control over, subsequently causing us to feel powerless. If I cannot control or change a situation, can I change how I perceive it and how I allow it to affect me? This is a good time to recite the Serenity Prayer: "Lord, grant me the serenity to accept the things I cannot change, the courage to change the things I can, and the wisdom to know the difference."

Personally, I hate traffic. But because of the amount of driving I do, it's inevitable that I will find myself stuck in it from time to time. (Actually, a lot of the time. I live in New Jersey. Need I say more?) I am able to accept that this is one of the downsides of my career. So when I am in my car, stuck in an endless parade of Fords, BMWs, and SUVs, I roll up my windows, crank up the radio, and exercise my vocal cords. My Honda is transformed into my own private recording studio, and I am the next American Idol! (Watch out, Simon. Here I come!) That I can deal with. I'm still not thrilled about my set of circumstances, but at least I am somewhat okay with it. I'm not a raging maniac, and that's something my fellow motorists are silently grateful for.

Identifying needs is critical and not always as easy as it sounds. Some are more obvious than others. As human beings, we all have the same basic needs: food, water, shelter, love. But there is so much more that we must attend to in order to feel comfortable and satisfied in life.

We all have the need for opportunity. Have you ever felt stuck in a dead-end job? You hated going to work. Why? Because there was no chance for advancement. Maybe your job was dull and boring. What is the unmet need here: to be allowed to develop and use your creative abilities, to be challenged?

How many people live with spouses with whom they are always angry? Does your partner love you *unconditionally*? Are you valued and respected *just as you are*? Is his love given to you freely and consistently, or are there conditions placed upon it?

Have you ever had a frustrating conversation with someone who just couldn't quite grasp what you were saying? Or perhaps he wasn't really interested in what you had to say and wasn't giving you his full attention. You find yourself getting annoyed and frustrated. You need him to pay attention and comprehend what you're saying. A need such as this can often be easily satisfied by simply asking the other party for his undivided attention, or perhaps presenting the subject from a different perspective. Surely he should be able to grasp at least one of the alternative approaches. If not, then perhaps you could ask someone else to explain it to him.

We all have the need for safety. It's one of our most basic concerns. Children live in homes where there's violence and then act out aggressively at school. Their anger at not having a safe environment comes out in a most inappropriate manner, time, and place.

We all want to be treated fairly, and yet how seldom does that actually occur? There is so much favoritism in our families, injustice in society, or preferential treatment at work. As hard as we try to be good citizens, do our jobs well, and be loving members of our families, we very often feel as though we are getting the short end of the stick. (*And* it's being put somewhere uncomfortable. Use your imagination.)

Have you ever felt left out, disconnected, as if you just

didn't fit in or belong, as though you were not important to anyone? Each of us needs to know that we are important and valued; we need to feel connected to one another. It's one of the most basic of all human needs. And yet there are so many who feel invisible or unworthy. That's sad. No, it's worse than that. It's inhumane. And we wonder why people are so angry.

There are children who have been abandoned (not just physically but emotionally as well) by their parents. It breaks my heart when I see a child acting out because Dad is nowhere to be found and Mom is too busy with her career or new boyfriend. This happens more often than people realize. With children growing up in single-parent families, being raised by grandparents, or in foster care, so many are getting the subliminal message that they are not important *enough. If Dad wants nothing to do with me and Mom spends most of her time at her job, then I must not be that important to them. I guess I'm not worth loving.*

To a child, as with all of us, time is an indication of importance. It's such a limited commodity and so valuable that we carefully choose how we're going to allocate it. The most important things in our lives get the most amount of our time. Where do our children fit into that? How many hours in a day are devoted *exclusively* to them? Think about it. The primary need of all human beings—and it's being denied to so many of our children. And we wonder why they're acting out?

And this does not end with the onset of adulthood. As an instructor at a battered women's shelter, I deal with so many women struggling with the pain of not having been loved and valued by their parents when they were children. Thirty, forty, even fifty years later, the pain is still as fresh as ever. When the need for parental love and acceptance is denied, it leaves lasting scars upon the heart.

As I sit here writing this book, I am deeply disturbed by the recent events that occurred at Virginia Tech, where a young student went on a rampage and murdered thirty-two fellow classmates before ending his own life. Investigations revealed that he had a history of not fitting in, of being teased and tormented as a child for being different. Not bad, just different. His need to be a part, to be accepted, to be valued, were not being met. He was filled with the pain of rejection and isolation. His pain turned to anger (as it so often does). His anger escalated to rage. And his rage was expressed in a violent barrage of bullets. Unmet needs became lethal.

The denials of certain needs may have far deeper ramifications than others, but all are important. Children also need guidance, rules, discipline, and consequences. These help to provide a sense of security and protection, safety, love, knowing they matter, knowing that they do not have to make decisions about their lives that they are not yet capable of making. All are profound and valid and need to be fulfilled in order for a child to be well-adjusted.

We need to be able to make mistakes without being judged or criticized. Have you ever made a really bad decision and then had to endure the ridicule of others? We respond with anger to their harsh remarks because it's not humanly possible to go through life without ever erring. We need to be treated with understanding and support when exposing our imperfect selves.

Do you have elderly parents or friends in your life who

have lost some of their independence? Maybe health issues are preventing them from doing the things they have always been accustomed to doing. They can no longer work or may be confined to a hospital. Perhaps they are no longer permitted to drive. They still need to feel independent, but that is becoming increasingly less likely. They become cranky and difficult to get along with.

I remember many years ago, I worked as a volunteer at Chilton Hospital. I came in one evening to hear the nurses complaining about an impossible patient who was in a room down the hall. Her name was Mrs. K., and she was screaming and raging at everyone. No one wanted to deal with her. I love a good challenge, so I volunteered (after all, I *was* one, a volunteer).

When I walked into the room, I saw a frail woman with snow-white hair lying on her back in the hospital bed. Around her head was a device known as a "halo." (I always associated halos with angels, but this was a contraption from hell.) It was a round frame that surrounded her head and was attached to her skull with bolts. It was then fastened to a collar that surrounded her neck. She was unable to move at all. I later found out she had broken her neck. I walked up to her and started a conversation. I introduced myself and asked her if there was anything I could do for her. "Yeah," she snapped at me, "get me out of here!"

I learned that Mrs. K. was well into her eighties and still living in her own home (without any assistance from others). She had managed to maintain the active lifestyle she had been accustomed to. A fall on an icy sidewalk had left her in a serious condition that could potentially cause permanent paralysis. Of course, the halo was intended to prevent that. But she was frightened and frustrated (powerless, helpless) and filled with anger as a result. She needed her independence back.

Was that a reasonable request given her age and medical condition? I didn't know. But I did know that she also needed a great deal of reassurance that she had great doctors and was getting the best medical treatment she could possibly receive. She needed comfort and someone to vent with. She needed someone who was willing to listen to her fears and not criticize. Could I provide her with those basic human needs? Certainly. It became a real pleasure spending time with her each week comforting and serving her as best I could. With me, she was respectful and polite, not angry and difficult. A small effort on my part had an enormous impact on her.

My advice to you is this: spend time alone with yourself on a regular basis to get to know yourself, to be attuned to your needs and desires, to develop a deeper sense of awareness. It is well worth the investment. At the first inkling of anger, stop and ask yourself, "What is it that I need?" We'll discuss this in greater detail when we explore the thirteen quick questions for clarity. Make absolutely certain that your expectations are in alignment with reality. Is what you're requesting fair and reasonable? If not, you may want to make any necessary adjustments.

And one more thing when pursuing the fulfillment of your needs: be careful not to put too many conditions on them. It will only stress you out if they are not met to your exact specifications. If I'm hungry and I need something to eat, technically any food will satisfy my physical hunger. If what I prefer to eat is not readily available, can I be satisfied

JANET PFEIFFER

with what is? Remember, the ultimate goal is to stop my stomach from growling.

May I also add that there is a difference between needs and wants? Needs absolutely must be met. They are essential for our survival and well-being. Remember years ago when doctors discovered that premature babies in incubators thrived when held and cuddled? Human touch: *critical* for our health and overall sense of well-being and yet severely underrated and significantly under-practiced.

I strongly recommend hug therapy. With the other party's permission (always ask permission and then respect their preferences), give that person a hug! Pretend you're Italian—*bon giorno*! We're so afraid to touch one another, and yet we all crave human connection. It can lower blood pressure, comfort a hurting child, calm an angry individual, and make someone feel loved. Try it. You'll see.

Wants or desires are those things that we'd like to have, but if they are not forthcoming, we will ultimately be fine. In fact, we might actually even be better off without them. If I want an entire new wardrobe, assuming that it is not because I have just experienced a dramatic change in my weight and nothing fits, is that really a necessity? No. It's a desire. I only *need* a reasonable amount of decent clothing to get by. The rest is a luxury. Keep this in mind. It'll make your life so much easier.

Enough about needs, we need to move on. (That's the last need, I promise.)

YOUR ROOTS
ARE SHOWING!

Anger is a very useful and important emotion. It's not wrong to feel angry, nor is anger a bad feeling. It is, in fact, necessary for our very survival. It alerts us to the fact that something is wrong and needs our attention. If I see a child being abused, I feel enraged. The anger indicates to me that there is a danger to the child and allows me to take action.

You see, when properly channeled, anger can be a powerful force to bring about positive change. The key here is in how we express it, manage it, and how we choose to use it. It can motivate us to do great things. Laws have been created because someone was angered over the unfair treatment of another human being. For years, people have watched our beautiful planet being polluted and stripped of its natural resources and have directed their anger to enforcing tough environmental-protection laws.

You have a right to be angry. You do not have a
right to be hurtful.

(You might want to highlight this. It's important to
remember.)

Anger usually progresses in stages, what I call the three *As* of
anger: Annoyed, Angry, and Aggressive. Here's an example:
I am bothered by something or someone. I find myself getting annoyed. It's the mildest form of anger. If I address and
resolve the issue now, it's fairly simple. If I don't, the level
of emotion rises to the second stage. It's more intense due
in part to the fact that the duration of time has increased.
The longer the situation continues, the more agitated I
may become. If I let this go on, I run the risk of becoming extremely distressed, and my behavior can easily become
aggressive. Be aware of what you are feeling from the get-go
(not gecko, the lizard that sells car insurance). Deal with it
then, and it's much easier.

Unresolved anger leads to resentment.

(I think you should highlight and remember this, too.)

Resentment is a heavy burden to carry through life.
Most people don't realize that what gets them angry
is *not* what gets them angry. Huh? That is not a typo, my
friend. Read it again.

Janet Pfeiffer

What gets you angry is not what gets you angry.

(Highlight this as well.)

Is that not the most confusing statement you've ever heard? Actually, it's an oxymoron (no, not a dumb bovine). An oxymoron is "a combination of contradictory or incongruous words."

There is a distinct difference between what triggers our anger and where it actually comes from. The external event (what we are seeing, hearing, or experiencing) is the trigger. Things happen. People say things. People *do* things. We have no control over that. We only *think* that that is the cause of our anger. But anger is a *secondary* emotion. *Underneath all anger lies hurt, fear, or frustration.* These are the primary emotions. These are the ones you need to be aware of and address. The event triggers one or more of those feelings inside of us. I'll show you a little later on how you choose those feelings as well and what you can do with them.

Too often we use the trigger as our excuse for getting mad. "You were mean to me." "I couldn't get the lid off this jar." "My husband forgot our anniversary." (Okay, that last one might actually be valid. No, not really—I'm teasing. It's still just an excuse.) Underneath the anger that I'm experiencing is one or more of the primary emotions I just mentioned. Let's take a closer look at each one of them.

Hurt: this feeling is primarily based on our perception or interpretation of what is being said or implied. We are often offended or hurt by another's unkind words. We mistakenly believe that words have power. They don't. A word is just a word is just a word, nothing more. We give them power by how we choose to internalize what is being said.

If I say the word *stupid*, it does nothing to you, right? It evokes no particular emotion. But if I *call* you stupid, well, that's a whole other ballgame. You might become irate. Why? Because we all make a crucial mistake that probably contributes to ninety percent of our anger: we *personalize* what is being said. "How can you be so mean to me? That really hurt." Look at one of the most toxic phrases in the English language: *to me.* That person's inconsiderate remark and lack of concern for your feelings is not about *you*. People who act in selfish or cruel manners are revealing things about themselves that are troubling. Behavior is merely an expression of what is going on inside of a person.

> Behavior is an external expression of an internal experience.
>
> (Highlight this, please. It's a critical point to remember … *always*.)

Let me give you an example. If I just receive word that my company is downsizing and I'm worried that I may lose my job, I may not be focusing on or even considering *your* feelings. I am completely wrapped up in my own fear. I'm angry and scared, and that gets expressed in the way I speak to you. I may be sharp, rude, impatient, critical, and sullen; you get what I'm saying. A valid excuse? Absolutely not. Fair? Of course not. Human? Absolutely.

My behavior is revealing something about *me*, not you.

(That does not mean to say that your behavior at that moment is acceptable, but that's a separate issue.) You may not know what is bothering me, and you don't necessarily need to know. You only need to understand that my (external) behavior is a reflection of my (internal) issues.

If, on the other hand, I am not particularly worried about losing my job (I have a hefty little nest egg to fall back on, or I was thinking about changing careers anyway), then my internal experience is completely different. I am more relaxed and maybe even a bit excited with anticipation about what is to come. This, then, is what gets reflected in the way I speak to and treat you.

Knowing that, you do not need to allow your feelings to be hurt. You can choose to consider that this is only my opinion, valid or not in your eyes, and that each of us is entitled to our own opinion. You can also learn to listen objectively to what is being said. Perhaps there is something of value to it. Are you behaving as though you are stupid? Are you not as intelligent as you think you are? Is it time for a reality check? Whatever the case, this could be a wakeup call for you as well. Or perhaps you are overly sensitive. Are negative comments hard for you to accept? Do you need to work on your issues of self-esteem? Do you need to be less sensitive? And what is this experience here to teach you? There are multiple avenues for you to explore that will reveal great insight and new understanding of the experience for you. You may also need to learn to forgive me for my lack of sensitivity. Otherwise, you'll carry that anger around inside and keep that pain alive for a long time to come.

So you see, hurt is a messenger. There is a lot to be learned from bruised feelings. Just like physical pain, which sends a message that there is a body part in need of help, emotional pain lets us know that there is another component of the self that needs attention. Search for the hidden weakness. Decide what needs to be strengthened. Work on that.

I have witnessed so much unnecessary pain and suffering be inflicted on humanity by our lack of respect for human life. All life is valuable. All life is *equally* as valuable ... in God's eyes (and needs to be in ours as well). And yet so many of us treat one another poorly. We decide who *deserves* respect and when we'll choose to give it. We say cruel and inconsiderate things to one another, and if people don't like it, oh well. We don't particularly care. It's not our problem. If they hadn't have been so rude, lazy, or selfish in the first place, then we wouldn't have said it. So, they got what they deserved.

This attitude causes so much hurt that is totally uncalled for. If we each made the commitment to treat all human beings with respect and consideration *all of the time*, we could eliminate a significant amount of the suffering that this world experiences. This does not mean that we need to put up with or tolerate another's bad behavior. We'll address that later in "Boundaries." Remember, people act out what they feel, and unresolved hurt can turn into anger.

Fear: this is another root cause of anger. My definition of fear is that it is a "lack of trust." *Hmm*, you're thinking, *I don't get it.*

Look at it this way: we fear what we don't trust. If I'm walking alone at night in an unfamiliar city that looks like a high-crime area and I encounter an unsavory looking individual sitting alone on a dark stoop, I feel nervous and uneasy. (Nervousness, apprehension, and worry are all forms of fear, only in different degrees.) I don't trust that I am safe at that moment.

If my coworkers are spreading rumors about me behind my back, I worry that my reputation may be damaged. I might experience some backlash as a result of their gossip, regardless of whether there is any truth to it. It may even result in the loss of my job, depending upon the nature and seriousness of it.

Even more than not trusting an individual or situation, I believe that at a deeper level our fear is a lack of trust in ourselves. We worry about how we will handle a particular situation or how it will impact our lives. *What if this guy attacks me? What if my boss believes those rumors? Will I lose my job? How will I manage then?* We doubt our own ability to handle those situations well, and we lack confidence about how we will deal with any changing circumstances should they arise.

Now, don't get me wrong; it's not always easy to alleviate fear. We fear the unknown. If I knew that I was going to lose my job, but would be hired the following week by an even better company, I wouldn't worry at all. I'd know exactly what to expect. But the unknown terrifies most of us. Why? Because we do not believe in our own abilities to handle whatever life has in store for us. We do not believe that we will find our way in our new circumstances. We doubt our own capabilities.

Look at all the hardships and challenges you have had to face so far in your life: you didn't get into the college of your choice; you were diagnosed with a serious illness; a loved one passed away. You did not anticipate any of these events, and yet somehow you got through them. Some of you even thrived as a result. So why do you doubt yourself now? You do not need to fear anything: financial ruin, discrimination, terrorists. Nothing! Whatever enters your life, you are already equipped to handle. Look at your past successes. That's proof enough. *You need to believe in yourself.* Remember the lion, scarecrow, and the tin man? They thought they had to go to Oz so the Wizard could give them what they needed. But he showed them that what they were seeking was already within. So it is with you. (I loved the scarecrow—he was my favorite. Maybe because I can relate … he needed a brain, too.)

There is, however, an even deeper element to this issue of fear and trust. The primary reason we fear is that we lack trust in God. We envision God as some lofty figure who sits on a cloud somewhere in the heavens. We are alone and must handle things ourselves. We fail to remember that God made a promise to us: he is always with us, and *within* us, providing whatever we need—strength, guidance, energy, knowledge. All we need to do is ask. Some of you already know this. I want the rest of you to consider seriously the validity of what I'm saying.

God doesn't give us *things*. God gives us *tools* to make those things happen, or to acquire the things we desire. He also gave us free will. I can choose to be successful in life *no matter what*, or I can choose to fail. For me, my strength and courage comes from my Father. He hasn't disappointed me yet.

Let me offer to you some tips for lessening the fear in your life. When it arises, stop for a moment and ask yourself the following questions:

1. What is the worst thing that could possibly happen in this situation? Try to imagine the worst-case scenario.
2. Is there anything I can do to prevent it from happening?
3. If so, what steps do I need to take? Let me get started now.
4. If the inevitable is going to happen, what can I do to begin preparing for it?
5. How can I lessen the negative impact this may have on me, my family, and those around me?
6. What changes do I need to make now (physical, emotional, mental, financial) to help me adjust better to the impending changes?
7. If this appears to be a negative event, how can I turn it into something positive? What good can come out of this situation?
8. What has this experience taught me? Remember, there is value in every life experience. We just need to be receptive to it.

Let me see how we could apply that to a real-life experience. Do any of you worry about dying? Maybe you have a family and fear that something terrible may happen that will leave them without your physical, emotional, and financial support and guidance. "What if I have a heart attack and die young? Who will take care of my wife and children?" That's the worst-case scenario. Okay, we've identified that. Move on to questions two and three: what can you do now to try to prevent that from happening? Well, quit smoking, lose some weight, get into shape. Check in with your doctor, eat well, lessen your stress, strengthen your relationship with God (those with strong spiritual connections often have fewer health problems), develop and maintain strong, loving relationships, research and employ the use of complimentary modalities to maintain good health. Those are just a few.

Eventually, though, we will all die, so there are no guarantees that you will be around as long as you'd like. On the chance that your worst fears will be realized (you've been diagnosed with a terminal illness), start preparing now for how you can lessen the impact on those who will be most affected (questions four and five). Write a will, take out a life-insurance policy, talk to friends and family about filling in in your absence, set aside money to support your family when you're no longer here. Encourage your spouse to pursue a fulfilling career in which he or she will be able to provide for the children.

Question six can lead to great family dialogue. Imagine having an open discussion with your family about death and life in the hereafter. It can be a very rewarding experience in which members can openly share their feelings, fears, questions, and concerns. Being able to develop a new appreciation for one another while you're still together can be a tremendous asset to your family. Easing the concerns of each family member as to how they will survive after you're gone can be very empowering for each of them. And if you believe in life after this one, then reassuring them that you're only as far away as a thought can be very comforting. Believing that you will all be reunited in the next life eases a great deal of pain and fear.

Question seven shows how any experience in life that appears to be negative can actually be the opposite. If you look for the lesson in dying, you have really hit the jackpot. Have you learned to live life to the fullest while you're here? Tim McGraw has a great song called "Live Like You Were

Dying." Get a copy and listen to the lyrics. They are powerful. I have written a book called *Jordan's Promise*, which speaks about facing life after loss. You might want to get a copy of that as well.

The purpose of this exercise is to help you to build your self-confidence by focusing on what you have control over. I cannot control a situation, but I can certainly control how I respond to it and handle it.

> "Life is only 10 percent what happens and 90 percent how we handle it and what we choose to do with it."
> This is a variation of a Charles Swindoll quote.

(You'll want to highlight this. It's one to remember.)

So many of us live *might*mares. We worry about what *might* happen. "What if" is always followed by a negative. So much fear can be averted by simply answering that question with a positive. "What if … I live to be a hundred?" See how easy that was? Catch yourself every time you project negatively into the future. Retrain your brain to focus on a possible positive outcome.

Retrain your brain.

(I like that one. Highlight it.)

When I was eight years old, I used to worry about having a stroke. I know; that is a bit bizarre for a child that young to be so concerned about. But what if I had a stroke and was paralyzed on my right side? How would I do things (I'm right-handed.)? How would I write? I was really worried. (That was in my pre-"trust-in-God" days when I thought I had to take care of everything on my own.) In order to alleviate my fears, I taught myself how to write with my left hand. People thought I was crazy. *Au contraire*! I knew exactly what I was doing.

When I was in my forties, I took a bad fall while hiking and broke my right elbow. When I arrived at the hospital ten hours later (I had to finish the hike—it was a really good one), the nurse in the ER noticed that I was unable to use my "write" hand.

"You can just put an *X* on the line if that's easier for you."

"Oh no," I proudly responded. "I can sign my name with my left hand. I've been practicing since I was eight!" She and her staff watched with astonishment that night as I signed my name as legibly as a lefty as I had when I was a righty.

Shift your mind off the negative and onto the positive. It's that simple. Well, it's not always *simple*, but it is possible and *absolutely necessary* for our well-being.

Be aware, too, that sometimes the fear is not emanating from the situation you're in at that moment. It may be triggered by the memory of a past event that frightened you. Let me give you an example.

Suppose you had been bitten by a dog as a child. Twenty years pass. One day, you encounter a dog that reminds you of the one that bit you. You immediately feel this rush of panic and flee for your life. This dog may be a sweet and gentle pooch who is inadvertently triggering a past memory of terror. Stop and reexamine what is really going on at that moment. Oftentimes, just by talking to yourself logically, you can relieve a significant amount of angst.

Several years ago, I found myself in the most perplexing position. I had stopped to fill up my car at the same gas station I always frequented, which was operated by men of Middle Eastern descent. I had always found them to be polite and felt very comfortable having them tend to my vehicle no matter what time of day or night it was. However, this particular evening, my experience proved to be quite the contrary.

I asked the attendant to fill it up. It came to twenty-seven dollars. I handed him a fifty-dollar bill. As he flipped through his large bundle of currency, he realized that he did not have any large bills to give me as change. I told him smaller bills would be fine. After all, money is money, right? He insisted on going into the small convenience store on the other side of the lot to get the proper change. I was annoyed, and he sensed it. As he walked away (he was only going about a hundred feet or so), I felt this surge of anger well up inside of me.

Where do you think you're going with my money? I shouted within myself. *If you think you're going to take my fifty and try to cheat me, you are dead wrong. I have a cell phone, buddy, and I'm not afraid to use it!* I held my phone tightly in my hand, prepared to dial 911 if necessary.

Whoa! Hold on a minute, Janet, I thought. *What the heck is going on here? This is not like you at all. You stop in this gas station every week, and you've never reacted like this. These people have been nothing but polite and professional to you every time. What is really going on inside of you?*

I took a deep breath. I examined my thoughts. Oh, my gosh! I realized that two weeks earlier there had been on the news a horrifying story about a young reporter from Pennsylvania covering the war in Iraq. He had been captured by the enemy and beheaded. It had been heartbreaking to hear. It sickened me whenever I thought about it. I am a mother. I have grown sons. How dare anyone commit such an unspeakable act upon a mother's child! I get very emotional when I view things through the eyes of a mother. And this was someone's child.

The gas station attendant visually resembled those who had committed this atrocity against humanity. Seeing him brought up a fear and pain totally unrelated to him. I had to think quickly. I did not like the way I was treating him. He didn't deserve it. *Quick*, I thought. *You have only a few moments in which to make this right.*

When he arrived back at my car with my change (which was completely accurate, by the way, and why wouldn't it have been?), I apologized. "I'm sorry," I said rather sheepishly. "I would have been fine with smaller bills."

"That is okay," he replied. "I wanted to give you back a twenty." We smiled at each other, and as I pulled away from the pump, I wished him a beautiful day. I left feeling content with the outcome. I would have felt horrible had I not made things right.

Pay attention to what is really going on inside of you. Look deep within for the real answers. Face the truth.

With the acknowledgement of truth comes
responsibility.

(Definitely highlight this. It's a keeper.)

Once you have identified the truth, you need to accept responsibility for it and for the way you behave. You cannot blame others or past circumstances for what you are feeling now. We'll speak more on the subject of blame in a little while.

Frustration: Frustration comes from the need to control. I want things to go a certain way in my life. As long as they do, I'm fine. But when things go awry (notice I didn't say "a pumpernickel;" that's way too corny), I feel as though I have no control (powerless, helpless). No matter how hard I try, I can't get things to change.

How many of you have worked on a project, and everything that could possibly go wrong, did? Do you find yourself getting a little testy? It's no wonder. You expect that if you do things "right," that you will achieve a desired outcome. Not always the case, my friend.

One of the most frustrating things in my life is technology. Designed to make our lives easier, in actuality it often complicates and frustrates us even more. I am not a computer wizard. (Now there's an understatement!) I only learned how to use one a few years ago, after watching my three-year-old grandson playing learning games and not having a clue what he was doing. Talk about humiliation!

My daughter gave me her old dinosaur of a computer, which I used for almost a year. *Not too bad*, I thought, as long as no one sent me an e-mail. (My friend Camille, however, had other ideas. She sent me several each day until I became proficient with it.) Then the inevitable happened: one day my old Apex passed away. I was forced to purchase a new one.

Okay, I thought, *I can handle this. After all, I have almost a year of technology experience under my belt.* So I purchased a brand-new, brand-name computer and hired someone to install it for me. I'm no fool; I know my limits. Now, do you want the long version or the short? That's what I thought. I'll make this brief.

Within the first six weeks, everything that *could* go wrong with my computer *did*. To make matters worse, tech support consisted of men and women who, although very polite, could barely speak English. They would instruct me as to what to do to correct the problem, but I didn't understand the terminology. It was a real nightmare. I spent a total of more than twenty hours on the phone with them before the problems were finally corrected.

I felt totally helpless. I had become so dependent on my computer, and as a freelance writer and author, had deadlines to meet. My level of frustration went right through the roof. I was so stressed that I had actually considered getting rid of my computer and going back to writing with my Ticonderoga #2s and legal pads. At least *they* don't break down. Okay, so maybe the pencil points break, but my old manual pencil sharpener handles that. No stress there. However, I am proud to say that I persevered and still have my desktop.

(And just one word to all of you who depend heavily on technology: *backup*! A week after I finished writing this book, my still-under-warranty computer crashed, and I lost everything. That's right, *everything*. However, I didn't panic [fear] because I had just e-mailed my entire manuscript to my secretary to proof. Fortunately, it was safe and sound in her computer, and when mine was fully repaired, she returned it to me intact. Remember questions one and two in fear? I hadn't prepared for the worst. This time I lucked out. God was watching out for me and took care of it. But I learned my lesson: always be prepared for the unexpected. Take my advice—backup. You'll be glad you did.)

How many of you have actually tried to control another individual? Come on now, be honest. I only see a few hands go up. If you're married, I can guarantee that you have at some point in your marriage tried to control your partner. Yes, I know, ladies; it's only because we want what's best for them. We can *fix* them and make them so much better than they are, and then they'll be eternally grateful and love us even more, won't they? I can see some of the guys rolling their eyes right now. You do know that you can't control anyone, nor do you have the right to. Right? (Say yes.)

Everyone has a God-given right to be who they are. We have a responsibility to love and appreciate all people exactly as they are. Remember, unmet needs? This was one of the examples I gave. Even if you think you can control someone, what actually occurs is more like this: you try your best to make someone do something you want him to do, or to be a certain way. You really pressure and nag him. At some point, he decides to comply. It's much easier than to continue to fight with you. But the reality of it is that he has made the decision to give in to your demands. His choice, not yours.

I can tell you this: as certain as I am that the sun is going to shine again tomorrow, if you try to control another human being, you will eventually destroy the relationship because the message you are sending is, *You're not good enough just as you are*. There is so much hurt that one experiences when given that message. And remember what the first underlying cause of anger was that I mentioned? That's right, hurt. Keep hurting someone, and there'll be an overabundance of anger in that relationship.

Earlier, I shared with you the first version of the Serenity Prayer. I'd like to offer you a second version to consider as well.

> Lord, help me to accept those *people* I cannot change, change the *one* I can, and give me the wisdom to know it's *me*.

Apropos?

After being divorced for fourteen years, I met and married a wonderful man. He's kind, respectful, hard-working, super intelligent, outrageously funny, but totally unromantic. (You knew there had to be a catch, didn't you?) Darn! I really wanted a sensitive husband to share long walks on the beach, snuggle up in front of a roaring fire on a snowy winter's eve, to profess his undying love for me in poetic lyrics released from the depth of his soul. Instead, I got Ty Pennington, Jim Carrey, and Albert Einstein rolled into a five-feet-nine-inch-tall stick figure. However, I was determined to change that. After all, it was my job, wasn't it, as his wife and all? You know, ladies.

So, how do you think I did? Take a wild guess. The eighty-seven percent of you that said you thought I failed were right. The harder I tried, the more he resisted. The more he resisted, the more frustrated I became. The frustration turned to anger and then resentment. I was not a happy camper. I wanted him to be something he was not, never was, and most likely never will be. I wanted something that was totally out of line with the reality of what he was capable and willing of giving.

I knew I was being unfair to him. After all, how would I have felt if he wanted me in the garage every weekend rebuilding the engine to his 1946 Jeep? Not me. No way. No how. I knew that if I wanted to remove this source of anger from my life (no, not divorce him), then I needed to learn to love and appreciate him *exactly as he is*. And you know; it's really not that hard. He has so many wonderful qualities. I just needed to remind myself of everything that I am truly grateful for in him. When I was able to do that, the resentment was replaced with joy.

Here are a few questions I'd like you to consider to help you ease some of the frustration you experience. Stop and ask yourself:

1. What am I trying to accomplish in this moment?
2. Is it realistic to think that under these conditions, with this individual and in the way that I want or need, that it will happen?
3. If so, do I need to do things differently in order to achieve this?
4. However, if my expectations are unreasonable and things will continue to be what they are, can I learn to be okay with it?

Acceptance of those things (and people) that I
cannot change is one of the keys to inner peace.

(Highlight this too.)

Many years ago, while I was raising my four children on my own, I found myself becoming short (well, actually, I'm already short). I meant short on patience. Trying to chauffeur my children to all of their scheduled activities and appointments was a bit stressful, and I found myself becoming somewhat of an aggressive driver. Don't get me wrong. I wasn't the type who would flip you the bird or run you off the road. Oh, no. I would just become extremely impatient and curse a lot under my breath. Okay, maybe not so much under my breath as much as out loud. Not proud of it, mind you, just honest. I expected that when I was in a hurry, I would be able to get from point A to point B exactly in my time frame. Think my expectations were a bit out of whack?

I didn't like who I was becoming. I knew my level of stress was out of control. I decided I needed to become a more courteous and responsible driver. I decided that in order to do this, any time I encountered people who wanted to pull out in front of me, I would slow my car down and let them in. One day I was traveling northbound on Ringwood Avenue in Pompton Lakes when I found myself approaching a local hardware store. Any driver trying to exit the parking lot into the southbound lane always encountered difficulty.

Sure enough, as I got closer, I could see a black and red Chevy Blazer waiting to pull onto the roadway. Practicing patience, I slowed my Honda down and motioned to the driver to pull out. As he passed by the front of my car, he turned to acknowledge me with a wave. I could see the driver's face. It was my dad! *Aww*, I hear you say. *How sweet!* It was. It gave me such a good feeling to know that I had made sure my dad was safe at that moment. Could I be willing to extend that same courtesy to other drivers as well? Yes, that wasn't too much to ask. It was, in fact, quite a small gesture, but it made a huge difference in me. With my change of attitude and focus came a reduction in frustration.

A little tip to help you reduce some of your stress:

When you're feeling overwhelmed by your circumstances, or with an individual

Cease, retreat, reassess.
Stop what you're doing—take a step back—reevaluate things.
Put things into proper perspective.

How do hurt, fear, and frustration create anger? Each of these emotions makes us feel weak and vulnerable. Someone's words have the power to hurt me, and I can't control that. There is a force that threatens my safety or well-being. I don't know what is going to happen next. I try to make my life move forward in a certain direction, but unexpected things keep happening. This isn't what I planned. No one likes feeling vulnerable. We all want to feel powerful and in control, don't we? Well, anger gives us that sense of power.

When I get really angry, people pay attention. People don't mess with me because they're uncertain about what I might do. Anger releases adrenaline, which puts us in that fight-or-flight mode. I feel a surge of power that energizes me physically and emotionally. At this point, I have what I need to respond to the situation.

The danger here is that too often, the response is one of aggression (we'll discuss this in greater detail further along in the book). Aggressive behavior is counterproductive. And may I add that it is not the only way to respond? When we discuss personality types and their corresponding behaviors, we'll delve into this more. There are other options available to us that will prove to be much more beneficial.

It's All In
Your Head

This is *by far* the single most important chapter in this book. In fact, it may be just about the most important chapter in *any* book … *ever* written … in the history of literature. Okay, maybe with the exception of the Bible. Well, actually, no, because the principle in this chapter is rooted in the Bible. So, that does make me kind of sort of right.

What I am offering you in this chapter will *change your life forever.* I'm going to give you the *key* to mastering your emotions and illustrate how that impacts every facet of your life. And as profound as this is, it is equally as simple. I am talking about the single most powerful energy in the universe, the force that determines the outcome of everything we do, the deciding factor that defines our health, happiness, success, finances, relationships, and more.

That energy is:

thought

That's it? you're thinking. *Thought? That's all she's got? All the hype and that's all there is? What a rip-off!*

Hold on, oh ye of little faith. There's a lot more here than meets the eye. Just hear me out. What you *think* is the most influential force in your life. Everything you feel, say, and do is rooted in *thought*. Every choice you make is based on *thought*. Every goal you've ever achieved or ever will achieve is founded in *thought*. Every relationship or career you've engaged in began with *thought*. Every emotion you experience begins with *thought*. It is the most powerful of all energies in the universe and yet one that few are able to harness and utilize. And yet without that, we fall victim to our circumstances and to the whims of others.

How often have you held others accountable for the way you feel? *You really hurt my feelings. You make me so mad I could just scream! You totally embarrassed me.*

We somehow believe that others determine how we feel and even *make* us feel a certain way. We believe that others control our emotions when the truth is that *we do*. Wow, what a revelation! To understand that all feelings come from thoughts is a radical new approach to living life!

Do you know what the world needs more of? Magicians! That's right, magicians. There isn't enough magic in this world. So I'm going to teach you all an amazing feat of *presto-digitation* called "TECO Magic." With the wave of your wand, you will be able to make any feeling disappear and another magically reappear in its place. Are you ready? Repeat after me (as you're waving your magic wand):

Thoughts > Emotions > Choices (Behaviors) > Outcome (Results)
Thoughts generate *emotions*.
Emotions determine the *choices* we make.
(We act out what we feel.)
Choices bring about an *outcome*.

(Double, triple, even *quadruple* highlight this!)

Let me clarify that with some examples:

Have you ever been driving down the highway when another driver comes right up behind you and rides your bumper? (I call them the enema drivers because they come right up your... trunk.) Then to make matters worse, they flash their lights. The message is clear: *get out of my way, lady! I'm in a hurry!* If you're anything like me, you immediately think, *Who does this guy think he is? Does he think he owns the road? Well, he's about to learn differently.* Our egos rear their ugly heads, and we begin a dangerous game of who-can-be-more-arrogant-while-operating-a-three-thousand-pound-weapon.

What I choose to think about him (or her—ladies can be just as aggressive behind the wheel), determines my emotions. I may be feeling threatened, disrespected, indignant, intimidated, arrogant, annoyed, wronged—you name it. My feelings then dictate how I choose to respond to him (my behavior). I slowly ease my foot off of the gas pedal and smugly watch as my speedometer needle begins to drop. *Ha*, I sneer to myself, *that'll teach him!* Teach him what: that I'm being a pompous fool, so insecure and pig-headed that I would rather risk an accident than to let him win? Oh, don't act so innocent. You know who you are. We've all done it. What we fail to realize is that that behavior carries a huge risk. I have no idea at all who I'm dealing with and what the outcome of this idiotic and dangerous behavior might entail. This driver could be mentally unstable and run me off the road.

Based on the fact that he is driving dangerously close to my vehicle, if I suddenly have to stop short, he could slam into my car. *So what, he hits me; it's his fault. I'll sue, and his insurance company will have to pay.* Except, maybe he's one of the thousands of drivers who doesn't have insurance. Worse yet, maybe when he hits my vehicle I'm thrown into oncoming traffic and hit again, only this time head-on by an eighteen-wheeler. Do you think about the possible consequences of your actions before you choose your behavior? Too often we don't. It's very difficult not to act out what we feel.

If I'm angry, I can try to control it, but it takes a heck of a lot of energy. What if I could change my feelings to something more manageable? Wouldn't that be easier for me, and better for both of us?

I do not need to know the truth about why this other driver is behaving the way he is. I only need to change my perception (how I choose to look at him, my *thoughts*) to change how I feel. What if, just go along with me on this for a few minutes, I decided to think that maybe he's in a hurry because he's rushing his child to the hospital after suffering a serious injury? Can I imagine the fear he must be experiencing at that moment? We've all been there; you get that dreaded phone call informing you that a loved one has been in an accident and has been rushed to the ER. You drop

JANET PFEIFFER

everything and race to be by their side. I know I have. When I got the call that my grandson had been in a serious biking accident and had fractured his skull, I well exceeded the speed limit to be by his side. In fact, I arrived at the hospital before the ambulance did.

A shift in thought changes how I feel. I don't need to know the truth at that moment. Giving the other driver the benefit of the doubt, I can generate feelings of understanding and concern. Those feelings dictate a totally different response from me. I move over to give him room to pass. I am calm and relaxed. His frustration from being behind me has eased, and a potential confrontation-turned-deadly has been averted. I arrive at my destination safely, and hopefully, so does he. See how easy that is? Magic, TECO Magic. (I'll bet David Copperfield can't do that. Well, he could if he bought this book and learned how. It's not hard.) Be a magician. Create *magic* in your life.

Thoughts generate feelings. They do not come from the experiences you're having. They cannot be controlled by another person. They come from within. That is the most important piece of information I could ever possibly offer to you. When you understand and apply this principle, it will dramatically impact every aspect of your life. Highlight those first four sentences. Write them down on a post-it note. Post them all over your house. Memorize them. Practice them every day. Make them an integral part of who you are.

Look at your watch. What time does it say? What is today's date? Repeat after me:

From this, the _____ day of _____, in the year _____ , at _____ a.m./p.m. and for the remainder of my life, I may never again utter the phrase 'you make me mad' to anyone. I now take full responsibility for my anger, and all other emotions, understanding that I choose my feelings based on what I choose to think. I no longer hold anyone else accountable for how I feel.

Doesn't it feel good to know that your happiness and well-being are no longer determined by others? Sorry to those of you who love being victims and blaming everyone else. I know I just ruined your day. But that's okay. Remember, responsibility is power. When you take responsibility for how you feel and behave, then you have complete control over yourself; no one else does. You are no longer a victim to the moods and whims of others. *You're welcome.* (Some of you just came to your senses and realized that I've given you a tremendous gift. Make sure you use it. I'll be watching.)

My first husband abruptly left me after thirteen years of marriage. I had been a stay-at-home mom of four wonderful kids for twelve of those years. I was devastated, to say the least. Talk about anger! I owned the patent on it at that time. I was hurt, afraid, and frustrated all at the same time. How could my high-school sweetheart do this *to me?* I didn't realize then that I was putting myself in the role of being a helpless victim just by my perception. It was many years later that I would come to a deeper awareness of truth.

My mind kept going to that place of fear. *Oh my God! How am I going to raise four children all on my own? I can't handle this—it's too much for me!* Every time I let my mind go there, my emotions (fear, uncertainty, insecurity, self-doubt) followed. I'd act out what I felt. I crawled into bed and refused to get up. I couldn't make decisions. My fear (helpless, powerless) converted to anger. Sadly, my children were usually the recipients of that anger.

My life went downhill. I couldn't think clearly. I had difficulty remembering things. I was sinking into depression. I knew, even then, that I had to change my mind set. I had to stop focusing on the fear and start believing in myself. The truth was that I had always raised my children on my own. My husband had rarely been around. So, in essence, I had always been a single mom.

Okay. Reframing my thoughts to what I was capable of managing gave me a sense of hope. I felt more confident. I got up and got through one day at a time. That, I told myself, I could manage. It wasn't quite as overwhelming as looking at my life in its entirety. *I can do this.* I repeated that over and over again. Fear: a lack of trust in myself and in God. I called upon him for guidance, strength, and assistance. He followed through on his promise: *ask and it shall be given to you.* As my confidence returned, my fear and anger subsided.

But the hurt was still there, and so was the rage that went along with being rejected. The fundamental need of all human beings to be loved (unconditionally) had been shattered. My first and only love no longer wanted me. The sting of rejection burned a deep wound into my heart. Only when I was able to begin to see myself as a valuable and beautiful woman, even if he didn't agree (and he is entitled to his opinion as we all are), was I able to begin to heal the pain. His opinion, though valid, does not necessarily constitute truth. God tells me that I am beautiful because I am created in his image and likeness and because I am his precious child (as we all are). That became a sustaining belief for me. Again, *thought*: *I am valuable and worthy*—a powerful message.

Finally, forgiveness: the force behind all healing, the energy that removes all residual anger from our hearts and restores wholeness, the ability to recognize human imperfections in others (we all have them; we have all hurt others at some point in our lives), and to make allowances for them, the choice to let go of the past. Inner peace replaces hurt.

And frustration: trying to make something happen that was not going to. For two years after our initial separation, I tried everything I could to get him to love me again, to get him to come home so that we could all be a family again. I even offered to convert part of our house into a private apartment so he could live in the same house as the children and me but we would not have any contact with one another. (My ulterior motive, however, was to get him to realize eventually what a horrible mistake he had made and recognize that he did indeed still love me. How naive and pathetic.) Obviously, that didn't work.

Gradually, I began to see that he had long ago decided he did not want to be married to me anymore. When I was finally able to accept that, I let go of the need to have things work out my way and accepted that divorce was inevitable. Although deeply saddened by that truth, I felt a great sense of relief. A calmness swept through my body, and I felt ready to move on. Once again, a shift in *thought*: *I am fine and okay with my new circumstance. I can have a good life—no, a remarkable life—even under these conditions*. I made the decision that I was going to rebuild a new and better life than I could ever have imagined.

And rebuild I did. My new mindset filled me with hope, enthusiasm, energy, and anticipation, and I began to do things that I had never done, never even *dreamed* of, before. My life has become infinitely better in spite of my divorce. Why? Because I learned that where my mind goes, my life follows. This is the essence of everything I've just shared. Maybe I should repeat it:

Where your mind goes, your life follows.

(Highlight this. In fact, *double* highlight it. And don't ever forget it.)

Thoughts generate *emotions*.
Emotions determine the *choices* we make.
Choices bring about an *outcome*.

Look at every area of your life. How's your health (outcome), finances (outcome), relationships (outcome), career (outcome)? Not happy with what's going on? What thoughts do you have when it comes to each of them?

Your thoughts create your reality.

(You know the routine here.)

I had a cousin who had a weight problem. She would constantly say, "All I have to do is look at food, and I gain weight." And she did, even when all she lived on was one container of yogurt a day.

When I was in college and dating my (now ex) husband,

I used to say that I'd rather have a bad marriage to him than a good marriage to anyone else. *Aw, how sweet! You must have really loved him.* I did, but I created exactly what my mind focused on, a bad marriage. Trust me. I learned my lesson. I am not making that same mistake with my present husband. (Did I refer to him as "present" because he's a gift? Probably so.)

Are you someone who believes that you're genetically pre-disposed to certain medical conditions? Be careful! There is an undeniable connection between the mind and the body.

What goes on in the mind manifests in the body.

(Highlight.)

I learned this more than thirty years ago when I became a student of the Silva Method (founded by Jose Silva). Today, there is so much scientific evidence to support this state-ment. Bookstores are filled with books written by experts such as Dr. Bernie Siegel, Dr. Deepak Chopra, and Dr. Larry Dossey. (I'll share my personal story a little later.)

Do we inherit medical problems, or do we inherit *beliefs* (*thoughts*) that in turn create disease? Think about it, will you? This is my own personal belief, and for me it is a very strong one. Anger is a feeling, right? And when we experi-ence anger, we can feel our heart begin to beat faster; the blood vessels in our head begin to constrict, causing pain. Sometimes if the anger is intense enough, our bodies begin to tremble. A physical response (outcome) to an emotion that came from where? A *thought*!

Worry and stress (feelings) can lead to ulcers, high blood

pressure, even a heart attack. *Thoughts*, generating emotions, can have a dramatic impact on the human body.

> When you master your thoughts, you control your destiny.

> (*Big time* highlight!)

Let's take a look at perception. What is it? It is what we choose to think, how we choose to view a particular person or situation. I was in Jamaica several years ago on business. (I know; it's a dirty job, but someone has to do it.) I had some free time one afternoon, so I decided to take a bus tour. The guide was a delightful local who had not only a wealth of knowledge, but a wonderful sense of humor as well.

As we were driving through the countryside on a sweltering August day, the air conditioner in our bus broke down. You never want to be on a bus in Jamaica in June with no AC, trust me. Some of the passengers were getting angry (lucky for them, I was on board) and began to complain about the problem. The guide gently responded, "Here in Jamaica, we don't have problems. We only have *situations*." She cheerfully began opening all the windows and encouraged her guests to convert their travel brochures into makeshift fans. Somehow we all managed to enjoy the rest of the tour.

> Life is not about truth or reality. Life is about perception.

> (Another highlight, my friends, and a great one at that.)

Is there someone in your life who is difficult to get along with? Have you labeled that person a jerk, idiot, loser? How does that make you feel toward her: angry, bothered, arrogant, superior? The way you see her will strongly influence how you treat her. You may ignore her, be rude to her, patronize her, or belittle her. I know some of you are trying to justify your opinions and treatment. Sure, we all form opinions and are certainly entitled to them, but have you ever noticed how harsh they usually are?

What gives you, or me, or any of us for that matter, the right to judge another? None of us really knows why that person is the way she is. We tend to be very cruel and unkind in the way we label each other. And that's just not okay. Each of us has a history filled with pain, sadness, loneliness, failure, loss, etc., and not one of us has the right to judge others for the way they are.

Hold on a moment, I hear some of you saying. *What are we supposed to do, just let people get away with stuff? Are we just supposed to let them treat us whatever way they want?* Absolutely not. You have a right to make sure everyone in your life treats you in a way that is acceptable to you. We'll discuss that further along in this book in the section on boundaries. And you don't have to like or associate with everyone who comes into your life either. I'm just suggesting that you be kind when you form an opinion of someone. It's the way you'd like others to judge you, and besides, you could be way off base.

You can choose to view that individual as troubled, unhappy, or struggling. That shift in perception will evoke a completely different set of emotions (compassion, concern, sadness), and your response to them will be noticeably different.

I have worked for many years at a battered women's shelter assisting the residents in healing past wounds and moving their lives forward. We have over one hundred and fifty residents, and many grew up in an environment where fighting and violence were a way of life, a means of survival. They are often disrespectful, hurtful, and extremely judgmental of each other. In most instances, they don't really care whether others like them, and they certainly don't care if they offend anyone. To say the least, they present a huge challenge to one another as well as to the staff.

I teach anger management classes as well as meet privately with many of the residents. To work with someone who is hostile, nasty, and sometimes just plain mean can be a challenging task. And yet, I am at my best when working with the most difficult cases. People often ask me how I manage to do it. "Easy," I reply, "I look beyond the behavior and see the beautiful child within who has been deeply wounded. When they're cursing, I see fear. When they're threatening to assault another resident, I see rejection. When they talk about wanting to ruin the lives of their batterers, I see extreme pain."

They may not know the full extent of why they are behaving the way they are, and neither do I. But I do know that not one of those women came into this world filled with all that fear and pain. Somewhere along the line, they were either taught how to behave that way, or they learned it as a method of survival. They can learn differently.

And I can help … but only if I pay attention to how I

view them, what I *think* of them, and how I choose to judge them. I will tell you from personal experience that the gentler I am with them (firm, but gentle), the better a response I get from them and the greater progress they make.

Perception: a shift in *thought* changes everything.

ATTITUDE, BLAME, AND PMS

Let's take a look at another interesting word: *attitude*. Do you know what attitude is? It is a state of mind, a combination of *thoughts* plus *emotions* (Webster). Together, they make up our attitude. And just how important is attitude? Let me illustrate. Look at the breakdown below:

A	+	T	+	T	+	I	+	T	+	U	+	D	+	E	
1	+	20	+	20	+	9	+	20	+	21	+	4	+	5	= ____

Each letter has a number under it. Do you know what those numbers signify? That's right, the position of that letter in the alphabet. And the numbers—what do they total up to?

You've got it: *one hundred*! Pretty amazing, isn't it? (That's no coincidence, guys; this stuff is *deep*.)

The importance of attitude is *one hundred percent*. In school, that's a perfect score. In life, one hundred percent is total, complete, whole. Attitude is everything. More important than age, sex (or lack of it, only kidding—that was meant to make you laugh), level of intelligence or education, nationality, or where we live, is our attitude. If I have a positive attitude, guess what? I can accomplish just about anything. Positive attitudes (*thoughts* plus *emotions*) cause me to pursue my dreams (*choices*) and make those dreams a reality (*outcome*). Negative attitudes can lead to stagnation or self-destructive behaviors that yield poor results.

And here's the good news (actually, it's great news!): you and you alone are responsible for your attitude. In fact, you get to choose it every moment of every day. Ever wake up in a bad mood (attitude)? Just as you decide what you are going to wear, what you're going to eat or not eat for breakfast, whether you're going to leave for work at six or six thirty a.m., or even whether you're going to go to work at all that day, you get to *choose your attitude*. If you don't like the one you woke up with, change it. Decide how you want to feel for the day, and then set your mind to that dial (just like your radio). *Today I choose to be happy and successful, and no one and no thing is going to change that.*

Then pay attention to your thoughts throughout the day. If you feel yourself slipping, stop and examine what is going through your mind at that time. Make any necessary adjustments. This takes practice, but I can tell you this for sure: once you have mastered this principle, you will witness an amazing transformation in your life. Every aspect of your existence will improve immensely. Not only will *you* benefit, but so will those around you. Give it a try. What have you got to lose?

Let's take a look at another important word: *blame*. How often do you blame others for what is wrong with your life? Most of us do. Something goes wrong, and we want to hold someone accountable (and it sure as heck isn't me). We're angry, and we need to direct that anger at someone or something.

There are several problems with this approach. First, we fail to recognize our role in what just took place. We have difficulty accepting responsibility for what we did or failed to do. We hold the other person fully accountable. That is very rarely the case, and unfortunately, it robs us of personal power. Remember, earlier I stated that responsibility is power? If I accept responsibility for my role, then I have the power to change things. It is extremely rare (and I do mean *extremely*) that only one person is completely liable for what has just transpired. Whether my contribution was at that moment or at a time prior to it, I have to be willing to examine my role and take accountability for it.

Here's an example: the first time I ever flew on a plane, I was twenty years old. My flight was departing at nine thirty a.m. I got to the airport at nine fifteen, figuring that would give me enough time to board the plane and settle in before take-off. Imagine my surprise (and utter distress) when I found the gates closed and watched the plane take off without me! *But it wasn't my fault! No one told me I had to be there at least an hour early.* And now, poor me, helpless innocent victim, I had to try to get on another flight. This was all Continental's fault! (Maybe I should have sued? Mental anguish, you know.)

But what was *my* role in this? Well, being a novice, it would have behooved me to find out either from a more seasoned traveler or from my travel agent what all of the particulars of flying were. So, I learned the hard way. Now I know better. And with all the airline security nowadays, I arrive three *days* early. I haven't missed a flight yet.

Suppose my adult child commits an assault on a coworker. Should I, the parent, be held accountable? After all, he's an adult and makes his own decisions. And besides, I wasn't there when it happened. Do I have any role in this at all? Maybe. Did I teach my child when he was young that fighting was acceptable? Did he witness my husband and I "duke it out" on occasion? Was I not present to raise him myself? Did I neglect to teach him the ways of peaceful coexistence? All of this needs to be taken into consideration. Keep in mind that this is not about blaming the parents or making them pay the price. There is no judgment. We are only seeking to gain knowledge and understanding and use those to facilitate positive change.

If you take a closer look at the word *blame*, you'll notice that there are two other words contained in it: *lame* and *me*.

How *lame* of me to *blame*.

(Highlight.)

Pretty clever, isn't it? I discovered that all by myself—a proud moment, indeed. Webster defines the word *lame* as weak. To blame is actually a sign of weakness. Taking responsibility is a sign of courage and inner strength. We do open ourselves up to facing the consequences of what has taken place, yet this is where our power lies. Blame renders us helpless, powerless, dependent on someone or something else. Let me mention, too, that responsibility deals with facts only (what I have done or failed to do); blame entails judgment ("she didn't get the report done on time because she's lazy"). Be aware that if you use phrases such as "I can't help it," or "It's not my fault," you're dealing with blame.

Refrain from blame.

(A good one to remember.)

How many of you would like to be contestants in my new TV show called *The Lame Blame Game Show*? It will feature pathetic moaners who will complain about how unfair life has been to them and how much they have suffered at the hands of others. Whoever uses phrases such as *to me, I can't help it, it's not my fault, she made me do it* the most often wins the grand prize: zilch. Now they can have one more thing to complain about.

The real tragedy about blame is that is damages relationships. For years, I have endured people in my life fabricating unsubstantiated falsehoods about me. I have been held accountable for everything that has gone wrong in their lives from their marital problems to their financial debt: for problems they are having with others to being accused of being something I'm not, for having ulterior motives for my actions, and for misrepresenting myself. Heck, I think the only things I *haven't* been blamed for are their bunions!

Don't get me wrong—I am not unlike any of you who have had similar experiences. My gut reaction is to defend myself because obviously the other person is totally wrong, and mean as well. I am, however, now at a place where I am willing to do a lot of soul-searching and thoroughly examine myself to see if there is in fact any truth to what is being said. I have even gone so far as to discuss the issues with a neutral third party who could help me gain deeper insights into myself. What I have learned is that those who blame are insecure and fearful and rarely have a leg to stand on. They are making a desperate attempt to divert the attention off the mistakes they have made (taking responsibility also means taking action to change) by holding the other fully accountable.

> Facing the truth about the self is the hardest thing one must do in life, but it is only in truth that we grow.
>
> (You may want to highlight this one. It is a powerful concept to remember.)

Blame may appear to be an easier path to take. But as I said earlier, it renders one powerless. I am no longer willing to be a scapegoat for anyone, and in one particular relationship, I have made the very painful decision to remove myself from this person's life until such time as the blame ceases and the individual is ready to face the truth. Hopefully, in time, we will be able to rebuild our relationship.

Have you noticed all the commercials on television for

diet products? One in particular, which shall remain nameless because I don't want to be sued, tells us that if we have unsightly belly fat, it's not our fault. It's due to having children, lack of exercise, poor diet, and stress. *Hello?* Is it just me, because if I'm not mistaken, I *choose* to have children, don't I? However, if you're a guy who's overweight, then what's your excuse? *My brother has kids, and he's overweight, so it must be his wife's fault, don't you think—since he didn't actually give birth?* Okay, I don't actually have a brother, but I'll bet there's some guy out there blaming his wife, instead of his Heineken, for his big gut because some drug manufacturer said his paunch wasn't his fault—it's because he had kids. Maybe it's actually his children's fault, so he should blame them instead of his wife. Hmm …

Don't I also *decide* whether I'll work out or become a couch potato? And what about how much I choose to eat and when I choose eat it? Am I ingesting food through osmosis while comatose and therefore have no power to prohibit it from occurring?

And stress: isn't that an emotion (and we all know where emotions come from by now, don't we)? Can't I choose to reduce the stress in my life by deciding to learn relaxation strategies? What part of all of this am I *not* responsible for? But some spokesperson whom I have never met tells me that I need a drug in order to lose weight. I have no ability to do that on my own since it wasn't my fault that I gained it in the first place.

Since it comes from outside sources, it needs to be remedied by an outside source, one that will probably cost me a small fortune and undoubtedly come with some serious medical risks as well. The sad thing is that so many are gullible enough to believe it. Without power, we are nothing more than helpless victims of circumstance (there's that word *helpless* again). And we wonder why we are all so angry? We're all filled with fear and frustration over the outside forces that (we *think*) are controlling our lives.

The Dalai Lama says:

There are no victims in life. There are only students.

(Highlight this, *please*.)

Let me explain. Remember early on, I mentioned that you need to remove two words from your vocabulary? Do you recall what they are? The words are *to me*: a phrase guaranteed to make you feel like a victim if you use it. Here's why:

Life happens. People say things and do things. I have no control over that. Yet the choices they make will often impact my life. *That's* where I have a choice. I get to decide how I want the current situation to affect me. I can choose to respond to it in a variety of ways. I can be hurt. I can get angry. I can allow my self-esteem to erode. I can allow my dreams to be shattered. I can become bitter and resentful. I can even plan my revenge. Or, I can feel understanding, maybe even compassionate. I can maintain my beliefs about myself regardless of what others say or think. I can become even more determined to pursue my dreams despite my new challenges.

Every experience in life has purpose. Every experience has value … even (and *especially*) the difficult ones. We've all had hardships in our lives. How well we handle them determines whether the experience benefits us.

By far, the most painful experience in my life was a long-term estrangement from three of my children. Out of respect for their privacy, I will not discuss the details of why it happened, other than to say it was not initiated by me. I don't fully understand why it occurred, nor do I agree with the way things were handled. But it is what it is.

Despite years of trying to reconcile, I decided to accept that this was the way they wanted (or needed) it to be, and I had to respect that. After all, just because I wear the title "Mom" doesn't mean that there won't be some serious problems in my relationships with them. I was not perfect (I know that's hard for some of you to believe, but it's true, my friends), and my children had every right to be angry with me. I also believe that there were some outside forces that contributed to the split as well.

In any event, you know that adage, "What doesn't kill you only serves to make you stronger"? Well, I found it to be one hundred percent valid. I was living every mother's worst nightmare: losing my children. We typically think of loss as death, but estrangement is devastating as well. (There's the added component of rejection, which causes pain—excruciating pain.) I had no control over their choices. I could not change the situation. I could not make them want to come back to me.

I trusted in God. (Hmm, fear: lack of trust in God, one of the root causes of anger.) I knew in my heart that there was a reason why I was going through this. I wasn't quite sure what that reason was. I blamed no one. I took responsibility, as much as I was aware of, for my role in it. Anger born out of fear was something I was able to avert. I believed implicitly that the experience was there to teach me something. I needed to figure out what it was. Coming to that awareness was not easy. It took a tremendous amount of soul-searching and gut-wrenching honesty to be able to face it.

I spent hours in prayer each day asking God for answers. He told me to forgive.

All of the people involved needed to be forgiven. I worked hard on forgiving. It is the final phase in healing anger. It is the force that removes any residual anger left on our hearts. It is the way to inner peace. To hold on to anger only hurts me.

I learned that every one of us is struggling with our own personal issues. Everyone is hurting. And we all express that hurt in different ways. Our pain, our fears, our sadness, are often acted out in ways that cause great suffering for others. It doesn't mean we're bad people. It just means we may be unaware of what our core issues are and unskilled as to how to resolve them correctly. It's part of being human. I know that because I'm guilty of it as well. I took out a lot of my own pain on others, primarily my children. My intent was not to hurt them, but I caused damage just the same.

I worked on becoming more understanding and compassionate to those who were contributing to the situation. Anyone who causes suffering to another is suffering themselves. And that is so sad. I prayed for their healing. I also understood that all people have the right to work through their own issues in their own ways and in their own time. It is not up to me to dictate how any adult should handle his own life. And while I do not feel that hurting another is ever justifiable, I do understand that it is part of our human imperfections. Everyone deserves understanding. After all, don't I want people to understand my weaknesses and not judge me harshly?

> Life is a do-it-yourself project. No one does
> anything *to you.*
> Everything that happens is *for you.*

(Another highlight, friends.)

Beware of self-pity. It is the guaranteed road to misery. So many of you suffer from terminal PMS. That's right, gentlemen, even you: "Poor Me Syndrome," woe is me, everything happens *to me.* Time to get off the pity pot. No normal, healthy adult is a victim. Life happens, and then we decide what to do with it.

I can feel sorry for myself, or I can look at it as an opportunity to grow. Personally, I chose the latter. Dr. Bernie Siegel (*Love, Medicine, and Miracles*), says that "there are survivor personality traits and we need to act like survivors and keep rehearsing until we get it right." This belief is not innate in some of us, but we can all *learn* to become survivors. I did. Very wise man.

I understood. I forgave. I also learned one of life's most valuable lessons: that people will think about you whatever they want and feel about you whatever they want. The truth about who you are and what you do has little, if anything, to do with it. (Remember, truth and perception?) How many of you know someone who's married to a loser? *What in the world does she see in him?* You can't stand him, and yet she worships the ground he walks on. Perception. Choice.

No matter how many attempts I made to reconcile with my children, I failed. I wanted to clear up any misunderstandings, to bring the truth (my truth?) out into the open. They were not interested. I had to learn to work *only* on myself, to be the kind of person that God is pleased with even if others weren't.

Whoever wanted to love me and share in that, would. And whoever didn't, wouldn't. I had to respect that. It was hard, but I did it. I no longer define who I am or what I'm worth by how others feel about me. I measure myself only according to what *God* thinks about me. Sometimes he's pleased with me, other times not so much. His is a much higher and more accurate standard.

I also learned that when God tells us that he will heal our pain (hurt = anger), he's serious. I was never happy with my circumstance, but I had made peace with it. There was, however, always a deep sadness for the severity of the loss I had sustained. That sadness remained a part of me until our eventual reconciliation.

Still, there was a greater purpose to all of it. Learning, healing, growing were all valuable aspects of what I had gone through. I came to know God on a much deeper and more intimate level, a gift for which I am eternally grateful. I could have been satisfied having gotten this far and closed the door on this chapter of my life. But I realized there was something more I was expected to do. It was imperative that I take what I had learned and share it with others who were experiencing the same situation so that they might learn from what had so benefited me. I had to bring healing to others.

I founded the first non-profit support group of its kind

in this country devoted to the emotional healing of those dealing with family estrangement. The group, "Reunion of Hearts: Reconciling and Reconnecting Estranged Families," helped families gain greater awareness of their real issues, let go of the anger, and heal their own emotional pain. The added bonus was that ninety-five percent of our families were reunited with their loved ones, *only* after they processed their own pain and anger and removed the guilt and blame.

Do you see how all of this ties into managing anger? We all go through unfairness and hardship. I cannot always control the outcome of the events in my life. I can *always* control how I allow them to affect me and what I do with them. I can stay focused on the injustice, the fear, the disappointments, the betrayals, the anger. Or I can switch my focus to what to do next.

How can I take this situation and make something good come out of it? What can I learn that will make me a better, stronger person? Those are profound questions. What makes the answers so powerful is that we change our focus (*thoughts*) from the negative (problem) to the positive (solution). By now, I hope you all have a new appreciation for the power of *thought*.

LUCKY
THIRTEEN

How are you doing so far, any questions? (Not that I could actually answer them for you, but it was nice of me to ask, wasn't it?) That last chapter was a lot to absorb.

Speaking of questions, this chapter contains the Thirteen Quick Questions for Clarity, designed to help you gain a greater awareness of your own anger, what triggers it, and what the primary or root cause is.

Over the next several weeks, I'd strongly encourage you to keep a journal. Every time you feel angry, no matter how slight or intense, stop and take about five minutes to answer the following questions.

The purpose of this exercise is to learn more about your own anger. You will most likely begin to see a pattern emerging. Eventually, it will assist you in either being able to avoid those situations, individuals, or thought patterns which trigger your anger, or to develop a plan as to how you'll handle them should they arise. The questions are as follows:

1. What is occurring?

Take notice of the events going on around you. Are you shopping at the mall during a huge holiday sale? People are pushing and shoving to get what they want before someone else gets it. There's lots of noise and rude behavior and kids with sticky lollypops in their hands. Pay attention to everything that's going on.

2. Who is present? (Not who *has* a present. Make sure you've got that straight. Otherwise this exercise won't make any sense.)

Pay attention to the individuals who are there. Does it always seem to be the same person or the same *kinds* of people? If so, what is it about them that is triggering your anger? This may be something you need to work on internally to correct. Do loud, boisterous people annoy you? Is it because you feel overpowered by their presence? Do you need to work on feeling more confident about yourself?

If it is someone who ignores you when you address her, this may be an indication that you need to speak to this person and perhaps set some boundaries. Or it could be a sign that this person is unhealthy for you to associate with and you need to distance yourself from her.

3. What is being said or implied?

Look at the nature of the conversation. Is it blatantly disrespectful? Is it triggering an insecurity or some unresolved pain within you? Is it humor disguised to hurt, such as sarcasm? Are you overly sensitive to the comments being made? Is it "constructive criticism" that is actually meant to belittle you? Remember, it's not just the words that matter, but the hidden messages as well.

4.   Is my perception of this person or situation fair and objective? Many times a simple change in perception changes everything. Remember the tailgating driver? Are you being open-minded and fair in your assessment of things?

5.   What have I said or done to contribute to this situation? What is the other party responsible for?
It is imperative that you be aware of and take responsibility for your part in what's occurring. Each party contributes something. Sometimes it's not just what we say but how we say it. Sometimes it's what we don't say, our silence, that can contribute to the problem as well. It may be something we did long before this event took place that needs to be considered. It may also be the result of something that we failed to take care of in the past.

6.   What time of day is it?
You will probably begin to notice that at certain times of day you have more tolerance than others. Mornings work for me, evenings not as much. When I get tired, I have less patience. I have learned either to handle things earlier in the day, or make the necessary accommodations as the day progresses. I take into account that my patience depletes as daylight wanes, so I make an extra effort to maintain my

composure during a given situation, or I will keep things as brief as possible.

7. Where am I?
   (It's ten p.m. Do you know where you are?)
I'm talking about location. Pay attention to where you are at the time your anger arises. Does it seem to occur as soon as you step into your office, when you're outside working in the yard, at your brother-in-law's house for one of his world-famous barbeques? Location reveals a lot.

8. What am I really feeling: hurt, fear, or frustration?
This is where you get down to the root of your anger. What lies beneath the exterior feeling? As soon as you can identify the root cause, you can begin to work on healing that emotion. The anger will dissipate.

9. What do I need?
Here is where a shift in focus occurs from problem to solution.

Remember that anger is about unmet needs. It is absolutely critical that you be able to identify your need at this time. If you don't, you won't be able to satisfy it, and the anger will continue. Be clear and specific. Don't attach too many conditions to it either. If you're hungry and you'd really like to have a pizza but all that is available to eat are cheese doodles, technically any food will satisfy your physical hunger. I've seen many people pass up the opportunity to get their needs met simply because it didn't fit their exact criteria. (Remember the line from that song, "If you can't be with the one you love, love the one you're with"?) They continue to suffer and then try to justify it. They are only hurting themselves, and so are you if you subscribe to this way of thinking.

10. Is this need realistic at this time, in this way, with this individual?

Many times, what we are expecting is out of line with reality. I have four children. If I expect that they will all do well in school, I'm setting myself up to be disappointed and angry. Some will do well; others won't. Some learn easier, and some have a greater interest in learning than the others. Each is unique, and my expectations have to be in alignment with who they are individually.

If I have a boss who's a control freak, is it realistic of me to think that she will relinquish some of that authority to me? Perhaps, but it's not likely. I may be able to gain her trust and cooperation in some areas that will make working for her a little more bearable.

If what I'm seeking is possible, then I must focus my attention on what needs to be done in order to make it a reality. What steps do I need to take, in what order, and when? Do I need any assistance, and from whom? Explore all avenues and begin moving forward.

11. If my need is unrealistic at this time, can I accept and be at peace with it for now? The Serenity Prayer suggests that we accept what we cannot change. Doing so soothes the feelings of frustration and helplessness. It allows us to redirect our energies to what we can control.

Whatever has not worked out according to my plans, am I able to make the necessary adjustments in my life so that this circumstance will not continue to cause me angst? Not everything in my life has to go according to my plans. Isn't that how we spoil our children, by giving them everything they want? There's a lot to be learned from sacrifice and acceptance. And most of what we think we need is really only a desire and not a necessity for the quality of our life.

12. How important is this issue *really*?

So often, we make mountains out of molehills. We stress and obsess over the most insignificant things. I was saving that last piece of pie in the fridge for dessert, and my husband ate it before he went to bed. I went ballistic on him ... for what? Is it really that big of a deal? In the whole scheme of my life and all that is really important, where does this fit? Put things into proper perspective. Most of what we get so bent out of shape about is relatively minor. I use the following as a gauge to determine if something is worth my anger:

Will I even remember this issue ten years from now?

If the answer is no, then I let it go. Highlight that question. It's a good one to remember and will definitely make your life much less stressful.

13. What lessons have I learned from this experience?

Don't miss the lessons! We've talked earlier about the importance and value in every life experience. Learn from it, and your life will greatly improve. Imagine learning not to sweat the small stuff. Or learning how to identify and satisfy your needs and reduce the amount of anger you experience daily. Imagine spending more time enjoying life and those around you. Imagine, improving your health.

There's a lot here to pay attention to. Don't miss it.

Look, I know I'm asking a lot from you but I promise—this isn't a life sentence. You only need to do this exercise until the process becomes second nature.

However, if you find it to be too time consuming, I'd like to offer you a reasonable alternative: the "Convenient Quickie Questionnaire," the six most important questions to ask yourself:

1. What am I really feeling: hurt, fear, or frustration?
2. What do I need?
3. Is the need realistic?
4. How can I get it met?
5. Would a simple change in perception correct this problem for me?
6. Is this issue really that important, or can I let it be?

See how simple that was? At least by answering the basics, you'll acquire a deeper understanding of what is really occurring inside you. And you'll still see a drastic reduction in your anger.

So, congratulations to those of you who have taken on the full challenge of the "Lucky Thirteen," and good luck to those of you who are choosing the "Swift Six" (try saying that six times fast!). Either way, I'm proud of you. Already I feel a growing sense of harmony in the world, don't you?

PICK-A-PERSONALITY

Ever wonder what your personality type is in regards to anger? Most of us don't. In fact, most of us probably don't even realize that there *are* definitive personalities. We can pretty much identify the way in which we express ourselves when we're upset, but there are corresponding dispositions of which many are unaware.

It is important to understand what our basic make-up is (I use Maybelline, myself) so we can have a deeper appreciation for the way we handle our emotions. I do want to mention that even though each of us may have certain traits that lead to particular behaviors, we needn't be held hostage by them. We can learn to overcome and replace ineffective tendencies with more appropriate strategies.

Let's begin by identifying the first three personality types.

A) Passive

People who are passive usually have difficulty speaking up. They tend to keep quiet so as not to upset or anger anyone. They do not like confrontation and will do whatever it takes to avoid it. Fear dictates how they handle themselves under these types of conditions: fear of what may happen if they voice their opinions, fear of how others may perceive them, fear that others may not like them if they get angry or disagree. "Peace at all costs" is often the motto they live by. Anger is held inward and rarely expressed for fear of the possible consequences.

Sadly, those who are passive by nature often get overlooked, taken advantage of, used, mistreated, or abused. They can easily be coerced and manipulated. Low self-esteem and lack of self-confidence keep them trapped in unhealthy relationships. There is also a misguided belief that "nice people don't get angry," and therefore, if I get angry, no one will like me. I'll be labeled difficult, a problem, obnoxious, or worse, and won't have any friends.

During the first portion of my life, I basically fit into this category. My self-esteem was so low that I couldn't risk disagreeing with or offending anyone and losing their respect. I grew up in an era where children were seen and not heard. I learned that I had no voice. And the times that I tried to speak up, I was put in my place. It became easier just to keep my mouth shut and maintain the status quo in my relationships.

I was also not allowed to get angry. Anger was frowned upon. I was taught that it was a sin, and it was not permissible to feel it. So I denied most of my anger and tried to keep the rest inside. To the world, I appeared to be a happy and complacent person. I kept up this charade for about a quarter of a century. This would later prove to be lethal for me as an adult.

If you fit into this category or know someone who does, please understand that the way these people behave is not an action rooted in kindness. I am not indicating that they aren't nice people. They probably are. I'm addressing the behavior. They act this way because they are afraid. (Hmm … fear—an underlying component of anger.)

I often hear the women at the shelter, when they feel they are being mistreated and are not standing up for themselves, say that the problem is that they are just too nice. My response to them is, "What are you so afraid of?"

They deny having any fear inside of them (fear, to many, is a sign of weakness). But after some soul-searching, it is discovered that they are usually concerned that if they speak up they will get into trouble. There is a proper way to share one's thoughts and opinions that can lessen the chances of negative fallout. They just haven't learned how.

Please understand that this is not healthy and can lead to a whole host of problems. For me, I found myself in an abusive relationship when I was in my forties. *Wow, an intelligent woman like you—how could you have been so stupid?* It has nothing to do with intelligence. It has to do with fear— fear of not being able to speak up, fear of retaliation if you do, fear of being alone again if he leaves.

Many years after my divorce I met a wonderful man, and we fell in love. After I was emotionally invested in this relationship, it began to turn ugly. All the warning signs were there, but what did I know? I had never experienced this kind of relationship before, although in hindsight, most of my prior relationships had many of the same underlying components. The major difference here was the physical abuse.

First, there were issues of control (fear-based). He needed to control every aspect of my life. He wanted to know where I was going, why I was going there, and if he didn't want me to go, then I had better not. There was a hefty price to pay if I disobeyed him. He didn't want me to have any friends, even my long-time female acquaintances. He limited my contact with my family and monopolized all my time. If I made any attempt to stand up for myself, he went on a rampage, and most often I was the target. Once again, I learned to remain silent. It was the lesser of two evils.

Not surprisingly, the fear in me eventually turned to anger as well. Fortunately, by that time, I was seeing a really good therapist who encouraged me to hold on to my anger and use it as a means of freeing myself from this dangerous situation. Anger does have a purpose, as I explained earlier in this book. When properly channeled, it can be a powerful force for change.

Let me clear up a common misconception about abusive relationships that many people have. Women do not necessarily stay with abusive men (and vice versa) because they believe that they *deserve* to be abused. Some might, but for many, we stay because we believe that they will change. We fall in love with their beautiful side (and they *do* have one, just as we all do). We try so hard either to fix them or stand by their side while they attempt to do it themselves. We *believe*, and we *hope*. We even believe that our love is strong enough to heal them, but sadly, it's not.

Often, too, we stay in abusive relationships because we have a deep-rooted fear of being alone. Letting go is terrifying to many because the alternative is (mistakenly) loneliness. However, being alone does not necessarily constitute loneliness. The isolation that occurs in relationships of this nature creates far more isolation than being by oneself. It takes a while before some realize that.

Letting go means moving into the unknown, and that can be a dark and terrifying place for many. Sometimes we feel that *something* is better than nothing, so we hold onto whatever we have. Hopefully, before it's too late, we can muster up our courage and take that leap of faith into a better life. Being willing to face one's own internal fears is crucial in being able to end a relationship of this nature.

B) Aggressive

Once again, we see a personality rooted in fear. While many, and especially the aggressor, believe that someone with this type of disposition has no fear, he is in fact, consumed with it.

Aggressive people have little or no concern for others when they fly into a rage. They inflict verbal, physical, or psychological pain on others. Their intent is to instill enough fear in others to cause them to back away or submit to their demands.

The underlying fear in aggressors is that they are at risk at the moment and may be hurt, not necessarily physically but sometimes more importantly, emotionally. By acting out in a threatening manner, no one will approach them. Most will either comply with their demands in an effort to calm them down or will retreat as a form of self-preservation. They need to be in control (based in fear) at all times due to a lack of trust (fear, again) in others and themselves.

If you look at the history of one who is aggressive, you will almost always find abuse or mistreatment of some sort. One does not come into this world automatically filled with fear and rage. What has occurred in this person's life that would cause her to evolve in this manner?

Deepak Chopra states that those who display extreme negative behavior have experienced some sort of trauma in their lives that they have not yet healed from. (Hmm, behavior: an external expression of internal issues—we act out what we feel.)

Let me give you an example. In 1976, I purchased an adorable little puppy, a black Great Dane I named Huggy Bear. (Isn't that cute? So was he.) He had giant paws and big floppy ears and like all puppies, was lovable and playful. He was the perfect playmate for my young children.

When Huggy was about three months old, I noticed that something was wrong with him. He had difficulty getting up from his bed. Sometimes when he was walking, he'd fall down and couldn't get back up on his feet. When I went over to help him, he growled at me. Eventually, he began snapping and biting.

I took him to a veterinarian, where he was diagnosed as having a rare bone disorder. The platelets on the end of his bones had closed prematurely, and he was suffering from a lot of pain. He responded well to treatment and was eventually able to walk again. However, the memories of the pain he experienced whenever someone touched him had left him very defensive. No one could approach him. The fear of being touched and physically hurt again was so deeply ingrained that he remained vicious.

It broke my heart when I had to get rid of him. Was Huggy Bear a bad dog? No, he was a frightened little puppy. He learned how to protect himself from being hurt and held on to that behavior long after the source of pain was gone. Biting was a learned response, which, sadly, he was unable to unlearn.

So it is with humans. People are not bad. They are not evil. They are *troubled.* They are hurting. They are scared. And yet we judge them so cruelly. How does that help them or us? It never makes anything better for anyone.

My abuser was not a bad person. He was a wonderful child of God, just like I am and you are. He just had a horrendous history of being abused. His father was a raging alcoholic who went on rampages, destroying the house and beating his children. He took the brunt of the violence in an effort to protect his younger siblings.

As a young man, he served in the Marines in Vietnam. He tripped a landmine and was blown apart. It took twenty-one operations to put him back together again. His body looked like a road map of scar tissue from the doctors' efforts to restore him to health. He returned to the U.S. suffering from post-traumatic stress disorder.

I met him shortly after he was released from rehab, recovering from an eighteen-year addiction to Valium. Any wonder as to why he was so frightened and angry? A lifetime of abuse and fear left untreated. Eighteen years of emotional numbness due to prescription-drug abuse. Years of suppressed emotions surfaced with no training as to how to manage them safely and effectively. His life was spinning out of control at the time

I entered it. His fear and anger were erupting like a volcano, and I was at the base. It overflowed onto me.

Do I hate him? Absolutely not. Do I think he is evil? No way. Have I labeled him a worthless piece of trash? Not a chance. He is as valuable a human being as I am. He is just deeply troubled. Which one of *us* could have turned out well-adjusted under those conditions? I know I couldn't have. My life was nowhere near as traumatic, and still I reached adulthood somewhat screwed up.

Please do not think I am making excuses for him or for anyone else who exhibits bad behavior. I am not. It is every human being's responsibility as an adult to reexamine his beliefs and behaviors and make adjustments when necessary. I don't make excuses for bad behavior—mine or anyone else's—but I do try to understand it.

And I am sharing my understanding with you *free of charge*. Well, not exactly free. You did have to pay for the cost of this book. But it has been an excellent investment, wouldn't you agree? Simply by incorporating this one new piece of awareness into your life, you can dramatically reduce the amount of anger you feel toward others who don't meet your standards of appropriate behavior. It affords you the opportunity to be less judgmental of others and more compassionate. A little understanding can go a long way.

And remember that what you *think* of people determines how you *feel* about them and how you treat them as well. *As well*: always treat others *as well* as you possibly can. I pray that you will see truth in this belief and adopt it as one of your own.

Many years ago, when I first began presenting seminars on anger management, I was speaking to a group of parents.

At the end of the talk, one young couple approached me. The wife thanked me for the presentation and said she had learned a lot. She had brought her husband to listen to me speak because he had a really nasty temper. I turned and looked at him. He said he was that way because of his father; it was what he had taught him. (He didn't know whom he was speaking to at the time. I *never* let anyone get away with lame excuses.)

I looked him straight in the eye and asked, "Well, that may be why you got to where you are, but what's your excuse for staying there?" I caught him completely off guard, and he kind of stammered. I informed him that he needed to take responsibility for his behavior and not hold his father accountable any longer. He was an adult now—time to stop blaming Dad. I think he got it.

Let me add, too, that even though I still see value in someone who is acting out badly, I do not necessarily advocate keeping that person in your life. Many times we absolutely *must* make the decision to remove ourselves from those people.

It was very difficult for me to get rid of Huggy Bear, but I knew that the safety of my family and neighbors was at risk. It was even more difficult to let go of my abuser. I truly loved him, but intellectually knew that it was only a matter of time before he killed me. Our primary responsibility in life is to keep ourselves safe and well. We can, however, let go of someone without bitterness or resentment. And certainly, we need to refrain from judgment as well.

C) Passive-Aggressive

This can be the most challenging of all personalities to detect.

Very often, those who are passive-aggressive do not recognize that they are. PAs have a lot of suppressed anger, anger that they may be denying or are completely unaware of.

They are indirect and underhanded; manipulative, coercive, and frustrating to deal with. This personality also has its roots in fear. Uncomfortable with anger and confrontation and also fearing the possible ramifications of both, they can be very deceptive when revealing their true feelings.

Do you see yourself as a PA? Do you feel resentment, jealousy, animosity, or fear toward another, but cannot bring yourself to express it openly? Do you hold it inside and let it subtly sneak out in the most undetected manner? You would probably be surprised to know just how much of your behavior is disguised anger.

I worked my way through college as a salesgirl in a small, local jewelry store. One of the other employees was an older woman. (Well, she was older than I was at the time. Now, I'm older than she was then. Yikes, now that's scary!) She and I got along quite well until I received a promotion over her.

Although she had been there longer than I, my boss gave me the position of assistant manager. It didn't mean a whole lot. My only real additional duties were to open the store in the morning and lock up at night. I was also to count the money in the cash register before going home each day. Not a very prestigious position, but obviously enough to create jealousy in her.

She began to undermine my knowledge of our merchandise. On one specific occasion, a gentleman entered the store. I approached him and inquired if he needed any assistance. He stated that he was interested in purchasing a diamond ring. I escorted him to the showcase where our diamonds were displayed. As I began to show him the various styles and explain the different qualities of stones, my coworker walked over and stood beside me.

"I'll help you with this," she stated to the customer. "I know more than she does about diamonds." I was mortified, but speechless! She and I had both received the exact same training on diamonds, and she was no more qualified than I was. So as not to embarrass the customer, I quietly conceded to her blatant display of jealousy.

Not feeling confident enough at that point in my life to approach her and discuss it, I spoke to my manager the next day instead. With both of us in her office, I explained what had happened, how embarrassed I had been, and how unprofessional her behavior had been in front of a customer.

As is typical with PAs, she offered a logical explanation. "Oh, no," she said, "You completely misunderstood my intentions. I was just trying to help you out with a sale." Well, what retail merchant is going to argue with that logic? Even though she was unwilling to acknowledge the truth, I knew better. It was not an isolated incident.

Pay attention to your behavior. Do you do things that are difficult to point a finger at, that you can usually bluff your way out of? Is there someone in your life whom you feel uncomfortable being around, but may not be able to pinpoint exactly why? Do you brag a lot, especially around those who have less than you? Any of these may be an indication of a passive-aggressive personality.

ACTING OUT (OR IN)

LIGHTS, CAMERA... ACTION!

So much of our behavior is habitual. We act out in ways we're not even aware of. Do you really pay attention to everything you say and do? Most of us don't. We kind of run on autopilot, making daily decisions that impact our lives and not having a clue why things aren't working out well.

We make poor choices that hurt ourselves and others without fully understanding what's happening. Until we start paying attention to the choices we make, our lives will continue to be less than extraordinary.

In reference to today's topic, let's take a look at the various forms of behaviors that correspond with the preceding personalities.

...rized by anger that is suppressed
...ften associated with a passive per-
...vastating consequences. We are all
...ion of depression: anger held inward.
Repressed negative emotions can cause a serious change in
the body's chemical makeup and can throw our systems into
a tailspin. Medical studies have shown that the body pro-
duces toxins in our systems when we hold on to such feelings
as anger, bitterness, resentment, sadness, etc.

We've all experienced some of the residual side effects of
repressed anger: upset stomachs, ulcers, a rise in our blood
pressure, headaches, muscle tension. For those who have a pre-
existing medical condition, have you ever noticed how anger
seems to exaggerate the symptoms? Doesn't your arthritis act
up when you're stressed out? Doesn't your bursitis worsen
when you become enraged with someone who's being hurtful
and mean? Self-mutilation, a deliberate infliction of physical
harm upon one's person, is also a form of somatizing.

One of my long-standing clients is a young woman who
suffers from multiple-personality disorder. I've been working
with her for the past eight years (not in a psychiatric capacity—initially it was to help her with an eating disorder). Over
time, I learned about her extraordinarily painful past: severe
emotional abuse, rape, incest, abandonment, physical abuse.

She learned at a very early age not to express her anger
because there were severe ramifications. As a method of survival, she learned to bury it deep within. But that didn't heal
the rage she felt inside. Unable to express herself, but needing to acknowledge her pain, she cut her arms with razor

JANET PFEIFFER

blades. The outward physical injuries represented her inner wounds. She could visibly see her own suffering and was able to watch herself heal. It became a symbolic ritual for her.

In my role as a trainer for the New Jersey Education Association, I work with a lot of counselors and nurses in schools throughout the state. I was deeply distressed to learn that many young girls use self-mutilation on a regular basis. It deeply concerns me that young people would choose such self-destructive behavior as a means of coping with their emotions. It also illustrates the fact that we, as a society, need to become more attuned with our inner selves and discover safe and effective methods of expressing and healing our emotions.

As I mentioned in the first paragraph of this chapter, when we hold on to negative emotions, it changes us physiologically. I am living proof of that. I have had three serious medical conditions in my life, and all have been the direct result of some deep anger issues.

The first occurred late in the 1980s. I don't recall all of the events that were going on in my life at that time, but I do remember that I was pissed off at the world. I apologize for using that word, but it was my phrase of choice at the time.

I'd walk around all day complaining that "this pissed me off," and "that pisses me off," and "he pissed me off." Everything bothered me, and I mean *everything*! And for the life of me, I don't know why I chose to use that expression. I hate that word.

I just want to mention here to be *very* careful of what *thoughts* you entertain because they ultimately manifest in some physical form.

The more I used that phrase, the more my body responded

to it. I told my body I was pissed, and it responded with, "Okay, I can do that for you." Guess what happened? I developed a bizarre growth on my bladder. (Piss/bladder, makes perfect sense, doesn't it?) It required months of treatment and ultimately surgery. Four months and seven thousand dollars later, I was free of pain and suffering … or so I thought.

I was still not over my anger, and two months later, the same medical condition reoccurred but this time with a vengeance. I scheduled another appointment with my urologist, who confirmed that the growth had indeed returned. This time, however, he wanted me to visit a specialist in a New York City hospital. Not having any health insurance at that time, the thought of spending any more money (of which I did not have an overabundance at that time) on a condition that I *knew* I had created myself, was absurd. I politely accepted his referral, left his office, and promptly threw it in the waste basket.

When I arrived home, I chastised myself for being so stupid and making such an unnecessary mess of my health. I vowed to use my mind to heal my body. If my mind is so powerful as to cause a medical condition to manifest, then it is equally as capable of healing it.

As a student of the mind/body connection since the early seventies, I certainly had enough knowledge and tools to utilize in order to facilitate a complete recovery. And that I did. With the use of meditation, visualization, prayer, affirmations, and vibrational energy, I was able to restore optimum health to my bladder. In less than a week's time, I had no symptoms whatsoever.

But I did know that symptom-free doesn't necessarily mean disease-free. So I returned to my doctor and asked him to perform another test to determine whether the condition was gone. He gently reassured me that it was not something that would go away on its own, that it required further medical treatment. "I know," I told him, "but please do it anyway. Just humor me on this one, Doc." He obliged and was shocked to discover that my bladder was perfectly normal! "Imagine that," I muttered, "must be a miracle." I left his office and have never had any further problems with my bladder since.

That was during my "pre-anger-management-expert" days. Even though I was fully aware of the impact my mind had on my health, I guess I had to learn the hard way. What, however, was my sorry excuse in 2006 when I ended up in the hospital with a kidney stone the size of Mt. Rushmore?

Early that year, I found myself feeling angry toward several people in my life: important people whom, I felt, were being very cruel and unkind. (Oops! I almost typed in those toxic words: *to me*. Good thing I caught myself before I committed a *faux pas*.) Let me rephrase that: *in my opinion*, they were not treating me with the same respect and consideration they afforded to others. I was deeply hurt and angry and decided I was going to stay that way for a while.

No one really knew what I was going through because I had kept my feelings locked inside where they were safe and could not hurt anyone. Because the truth is that if I were to express the depth of my pain at that time, I could have inflicted some serious verbal harm on several people. While I advocate being truthful with others and discussing what is bothering us, there are also times when it is perfectly acceptable to remain silent while we resolve within ourselves the issues that are causing us grief. (*Resolve*, not suppress—remember that.)

However, that was not the case with me. I had made up my mind that I wanted to be angry, and no one was going to deny me my feelings, no matter what the risk. I figured that as long as I didn't use the term "pissed off" again, I should be okay. Wrong!

Anger is anger, and my body responded just as strongly. After about five months of engaging in a daily internal rampage, one of my kidneys rebelled. I awoke one afternoon from a nap in excruciating pain. Long story short: I had a nine-millimeter kidney stone that required surgery. I was prescribed serious pain medication, which at times was completely ineffective. I endured severe discomfort for several more months, lost time at work, and accrued enormous medical expenses. Think I've learned my lesson this time? I sincerely hope so. That last experience was a nightmare.

In a recent e-mail from Dr. Siegel, he says that,

> "One's life and one's health are inseparable. Genes do not make the decisions. Our internal environment does. You internalize anger and it destroys you. Self-induced healing is not an accident."

Internal environment: I'm keeping mine hospitable from now on.

Look at your own health. How much of it can be linked to undetected or unresolved anger? Louise Hay (*Heal Your Body: The Mental Causes for Physical Illnesses and the Metaphysical Way to Overcome Them*) is in my opinion one of the most knowledgeable authors on the planet when it comes to this subject. Thanks in part to her expertise, I have a much greater understanding of what emotional issues lie beneath my medical conditions and am able to address and resolve them as a result. I would strongly recommend that you read her book. Check out any medical conditions you may be suffering from and learn about the underlying emotional cause. Once you understand the connection, you will have much greater influence over your health.

Be aware that physical maladies are not the only expression of somatizing. Eating disorders are often a manifestation of internalized anger. For more than ten years, I suffered from bulimia, an emotional disorder rooted deeply in suppressed anger. A lifetime of stuffing my emotions led to a decade of binging and purging—a physical expression of stuffing my feelings and then cleansing them by vomiting. This behavior can have serious and permanent effects on an individual's health. In some cases it can lead to death.

If you are one who tends to keep your feelings buried deep within and are suffering the consequences, I strongly urge you to begin to get in touch with your emotions. If necessary, enlist the aid of a trusted therapist. Know that every feeling is valid and beneficial. Feelings are not bad, nor should they be denied. All have a place in your life. They can reveal important information about you and the issues you are struggling with. The deciding factor that determines whether an emotion is beneficial or detrimental is the way in which you choose to process and use it.

Here's an activity that you can practice to help get in touch with and safely release your feelings. It's called The

Write Approach to Anger. Basically, it's a form of journaling. Whenever you are experiencing a feeling that you are uncomfortable with, take out a notebook and write down what that feeling is. This is your own personal journal, not to be shared with anyone unless you so choose.

Write about the experience you are having and what feelings are associated with it. Give yourself permission to feel what you feel. Write it all down. Look for a deeper understanding behind the initial emotion. If I'm feeling hurt, is that an indication that what I'm really feeling is unimportant, insignificant? That's what you need to work on: the real feeling, the root, the bottom line.

Feelings give us great insight into ourselves: who we are, what's important to us, what our core issues are. Once I understand what I'm really dealing with, it becomes much easier to manage. If I'm feeling unimportant, what can I do to boost my self-esteem? My focus shifts from pain and fear (problem) to feeling good about myself (solution). Then I can begin to take those steps necessary to raise my self-image.

Write down those steps. Follow through on each one. Keep a record of the effect of each behavior for future reference. Repeat those that have proven to be most beneficial.

Also, I want you to delay any negative behaviors for ten minutes while you pursue taking positive steps toward the solution. Usually what will happen is that after the initial ten minutes, the desire to inflict suffering on yourself diminishes enough so that you are less likely to act upon it. And the more you practice this behavior, the less inclined you are to hurt yourself. You have replaced a negative behavior with one that is positive and beneficial.

JANET PFEIFFER

Aa) Self-Punishing

Did you notice that this section is also prefixed with the letter *a*? That is not an error. Both somatizing and self-punishing behaviors are linked to passive personalities. Self-punishing, however, focuses on self-blame, holding oneself fully accountable for the other party and how he is feeling and acting. You've heard people blame themselves for what another person is experiencing: "I really hurt Jimmy's feelings"; "My wife was in a good mood until I came home and ruined it"; "I totally embarrassed my coworker today." Does that sound like anyone you know? Does it sound like you?

Please understand that you are not responsible for another person's feelings. You can't be. If what I said earlier is true (and it is), then every person is responsible for his own feelings. Feelings come from *thoughts*. Each individual chooses his own *thoughts* and therefore determines how he will feel.

I cannot make anyone feel anything. I am not responsible for anyone's life: happiness, sadness, successes, failures. I am only accountable for my own.

Let me make something perfectly clear because I can just hear some of you saying, "Oh, good, now I can say whatever I want, and if someone doesn't like it, oh well! It's not my fault if their feelings get hurt. Janet just said so." No, Janet did not say that. While I did say that every person chooses his own feelings, that does not give any of us the right to disregard how our words may impact him.

We have a moral and ethical responsibility to take into consideration how the other party may be affected by what we say and do. Not everyone has the understanding of the key principle of *thought*. Kindness, concern, and compassion are absolutely crucial for all healthy relationships. And even though you are now armed with the knowledge that no one can hurt your feelings or make you angry, don't you still want others to speak to you politely and with consideration? *Do unto others . . .* right?

So before I say or do anything, I need to ask myself, "How might the other party feel if I say or do this?" If I think that she might become hurt or angry, then perhaps I need to rethink my words and actions and choose a better alternative. It's called "being considerate of," not "being responsible for."

If you are someone who continually blames yourself for the way others feel, this will gradually erode your self-esteem and subject you to unnecessary stress. Feeling as though it is your fault whenever someone feels bad will make you feel worse about yourself. Eventually, you may end up feeling worthless and doubt your own value. *I'm a big screw-up. I can't do anything right.*

Low self-esteem leads to a whole host of other problems, including lack of enthusiasm for life, poor career choices, lower-paying jobs, depression, unhealthy relationships, and more. We talked about blame in a previous chapter. Refer back to it to refresh your memory if necessary. And please remember: you do not have that kind of power over anyone. Some may try to coerce you into believing that you have caused them pain. You haven't.

I would like you to practice the following exercise to reverse the self-punishing pattern:

When an event occurs and you feel totally responsible and begin blaming yourself, get out a piece of paper. Make two columns. Put your name at the top of the first column and the other party's name on the second. Then list everything that you said or did that contributed to the situation. List in the second column what the other party said or did or failed to say or do. Deal with facts only. Do not include judgments or criticisms.

Next, go over the list and review what you have written. Is it accurate? Do you need to make any changes? If so, do that now.

Then reread the list under your name. What did you do? Why did you do those things? Was it with the intention of hurting the other person and making matters worse? Did you act without having the proper knowledge you needed in order to be able to handle things better? What did you think the outcome would be? How could you have handled things better? Can you go back and correct your mistakes? If so, follow through on that.

Vow to learn from those mistakes and not repeat them. Forgive yourself for handling things poorly. Make sure the other party understands what you are willing to be held accountable for and what you won't, even if he refuses to accept his share of the responsibility. Hold fast to what you believe.

Then repeat positive affirmations about yourself. Work on building a healthy sense of self. Discover your intrinsic value, and never allow anyone to rob you of that. You are as wonderful and valuable a person as everyone else. Believe in your own beauty.

B) Explosive

Are you someone who yells, curses, throws things, punches walls, or slams doors? Do you threaten others, physically attack them, or resort to verbal assaults? Of course not! But you probably know someone who is, and you'd really like to help them, wouldn't you? I knew it because that's the kind of person you are, always willing to help others. You're a wonderful friend.

So this person you know: does she act tough and fearless? Would you please tell her for me that I don't buy it for a minute? She is not tough at all. This behavior is rooted in fear. (Remember the aggressive personality? This is the corresponding behavior.) Aggressive behavior puts the other person on the defensive because they themselves feel unsafe.

On some level, they believe that the other party is the enemy, able to hurt them in some capacity. This could be the result of prior experiences they've had that taught them that people are not trustworthy and that one must keep a guard up at all times. Like Huggy Bear, they act in a hostile manner as a method of self-protection from a *perceived* threat, even if the threat is not real.

This behavior shows a complete lack of respect and concern for the safety and well-being of the other party. One who engages in explosive anger is totally self-absorbed and has no regard for the feelings of the other. He goes into survival mode and uses whatever tactics necessary in order to keep himself safe. You can almost smell his fear. (I wonder if fear smells bad. I'm guessing it does.)

Remember what I said about fear: a lack of trust. Even if the opposing party is not trustworthy, the real issue here is the lack of faith the aggressor has in his own ability to handle the situation effectively without resorting to hostility. I'll show you what I mean a little later on when I talk about assertiveness and boundaries.

I feel reasonably confident that if you're reading this book, you are not an aggressive person who blows up when you become angry. Very few who are, are willing to acknowledge that they need to work on themselves in this area. They will usually offer a lame statement such as, "Well, if my wife would stop getting me so angry, I wouldn't have to hit her!" (Lame-blame: remember, feelings come from *thoughts*.) Or how about this one: "It's better to let it out than to hold it in!" Well, yes and no. It is healthier to release the anger, but *how* you do it is of great importance.

Explosive anger can lead to serious medical problems. Have any of you ever witnessed, or heard about, someone getting so angry they actually suffered a heart attack? Many years ago, Stanford University did a study and found that those who expressed their anger in this manner were at a higher risk for developing blood clots to the heart. We all know that one clot can be fatal.

CBS News reported on August 30, 2006, that there was a recent medical study indicating that middle-aged men with long-standing anger and hostility show a faster age-related decline in lung power. Hostility and anger have been linked with cardiovascular disease, asthma, and death in other studies as well.

Remember my abuser? I spoke about his fear of being hurt (fear and hurt: root causes of anger, and here we have the two combined). His story is a prime example of the underlying fear behind his angry outbursts. Earlier in this book I mentioned that anger makes us feel powerful. (The roots of anger—hurt, fear, and frustration—have the opposite effect on us. They generate feelings of *powerlessness*.)

By acting out aggressively, I delude myself into feeling as though I'm in control when it's the opposite that is true. I am, in fact, *reacting* to the situation I'm in or to the other person. I am not *acting* logically. In truth, I am not in control. My buttons are being pushed, and I am responding automatically.

However, we do tend to pay attention to people when they're out of control. Their behavior is frightening and very often we'll concede to appease them. This gives the illusion that they are causing us to behave in a certain manner, when in fact we are making that decision ourselves in order to avoid any further outburst from them. To say or do anything that could possibly cause their anger to intensify is scary and extremely foolish. Therefore, I make what I believe to be the best decision at that moment.

Would it be safe for me to say that most of us have behaved really badly at some point in our lives? I know I have. I did mention that for the early part of my life I was basically a passive person. However, that all changed when I was a young mother in my twenties. Having four children, by choice, in five years was a bit overwhelming. Okay, it was *way* overwhelming!

When my husband and I decided to become parents, I believed that he would be by my side helping me care for our babies. How naïve. (Unrealistic expectation.) He spent the majority of his time at his job, and I was left alone most of the time. I was lonely, sad, hurt, tired, and very frustrated. Taking care of that many small children on my own, with no training in parenting, was much more than I could handle.

The expectations of marriage and motherhood when I began that chapter in my life were not realistic. Remember how I talked about expectations and unmet needs in relation to anger? My needs as a wife and woman were not being satisfied. My husband was inattentive and absent. My expectations of my ability to be a patient and perfect mother were grandiose. The pain of being in a bad marriage coupled with the frustration of trying to take care of four small children was too much for me. I felt as though my life was spinning out of control.

I was trying to get my children to behave according to the way I needed them to. They were more interested in acting in a way that suited them. It seemed to me that the only way I could control them was with rage. Why did I think that the louder I yelled and the more I threatened, the more they would comply with my demands? They didn't. I caused a lot of pain to my children and a great deal of suffering and damage to my family. This is the deepest regret I have in my life.

The pain I caused them eventually turned to anger inside them as well. A vicious cycle of hurt and anger: I fell into the self-punishing mode and blamed myself exclusively for the mess my family was in. So did my husband.

Thankfully, I had a wonderful therapist who helped me put things into perspective and relinquish some of the liability to others. With a greater understanding of the truth, I was then able to begin taking some positive steps toward becoming a better mother. However, the damage had already been done, and once the wounds have been inflicted, they can take years to heal. Very often, they leave lasting scars. Anyone who has been abused will tell you that the verbal and emotional wounds are infinitely more difficult to heal than the physical.

C) Passive-Aggressive

Has anyone ever teased you about something you don't find amusing? Are you self-conscious about losing your hair, and yet your friends tell bald jokes in your presence? When you become offended, do they tell you to lighten up? After all, they're only kidding. "What's wrong with you? Can't you take a joke? Everyone else thought it was hysterical."

This is a classic example of passive-aggressive behavior. It is behavior that is intended to hurt, offend, embarrass, or humiliate, but is often disguised as humor. It's those little "digs" that someone makes, those off-color remarks, the sarcasms that sting, that are anger disguised as something else. It's a cowardly way of releasing anger, yet not having to own up to it and face the consequences.

People will often pretend to be nice by offering their unsolicited opinion of you so that you can know the "truth" about who you are. You know that it's only because they care, right? Someone might say, "You're just lazy. That's why you never get your work done on time." *Oh, really? Am I lazy, or is that just your opinion? Do you know the real reasons why I don't complete my tasks in the prescribed amount of time? Did you bother to ask me and find out why this happens? Maybe I just work at a slower pace than the rest of the world. And what would even make you think I needed to know? What makes you think I don't already possess this knowledge and have either chosen to accept that this is the way I am, or have decided to make the nec-essary changes to improve?*

What is the motive behind that statement? Motive is key. If I am your supervisor at work and feel that your job may be at risk, or that you are putting a project in jeopardy as a result of the way you work, then it is my responsibility to make sure that things turn out in the best way possible. In this case, my motives for speaking to you are honorable. If I am a coworker and have no concern for your well-being and am not willing to assist you in making some positive changes that will ben-efit you, then perhaps my reason for making this statement is questionable. Be wary of those who engage in "constructive criticism." It is often not constructive at all. It is simply *a cloak of concern draped over a base of anger.* (Ooh, I like that one. You can highlight that if you'd like, especially if it applies.)

> Constructive criticism is often a cloak of concern
> draped over a base of anger.

Do you participate in gossip, either as a writer (one who fab-ricates it initially), a messenger (one who delivers and spreads it), or a receiver (one who actively listens)? What is your motive for talking about someone else, whether the informa-tion you are sharing is valid or not? If you found out that your neighbor was having an affair, would you tell others about it? If so, why? Is it so that the two of you could intervene and help the engaging parties come to their senses before someone gets hurt? Or do you view this as an opportunity to make her look bad, perhaps damage her reputation, or ruin her marriage once her husband finds out? "Everyone gossips, and besides, if people don't want others talking about them behind their backs, then they shouldn't be doing stuff like that. It's their own fault. If they can do it, we can talk about it."

If you have ever had a rumor spread about you, then you know how devastating it can be. Rumors can cause extensive and irreparable damage to those involved and extend way beyond. Innocent parties have suffered immeasurable harm that can take a lifetime to repair. I have personally seen lives destroyed because of vicious gossip. And those spreading it cared little, if any, about the impact it would have on the parties involved. If you look closely, you'll find an undercurrent of anger behind the vicious comments.

Many years ago, I was the object of a nasty and destructive rumor that was totally without merit. The person who initiated the rumor was consumed with anger toward me. My success in life had spurred a jealousy that turned into vindictiveness. In an effort to discredit me, tarnish my reputation, and destroy some of my most cherished relationships, this person fabricated some disturbing lies about me.

It ultimately caused a significant amount of unnecessary suffering for me as well as for many innocent people. The damage was extensive and long-lasting. Had this person had the courage to face the truth about the real cause of the anger and resolve it, this tragic situation could have been avoided. And the frightening thing is that this person believes that the statements made were perfectly justified and founded in truth. The danger is that this may very well happen again. People who do not acknowledge passive-aggressive anger are destined to repeat it.

Have you ever known people who were chronically late?

This may be a form of passive-aggressive behavior. It's their way of gaining control, especially if they know it bothers you. Of course, it's never their fault: the alarm clock didn't go off, there was a lot of traffic, they couldn't find their favorite pair of shoes, yada, yada, yada. The simple fact is that if their lives depended on being on time, there would be no excuses.

Do you see how subtle this can be? You first need to recognize this behavior in yourself and vow to make some changes. Then, you have permission to notice it in others. Just remember, this book is about the self—*you*—first and foremost. Everyone else is secondary. Read on.

Do you hold on to the things people did years ago? Do you refuse to move out of the past and into the present? Do you bring up these incidents and hold them over other people's heads? "I'll never forget when you embarrassed me in front of the entire fifth-grade class." "You know, I would never say anything like that to you." "I'll never forgive you for what you did." These kinds of statements are intended to inflict guilt and shame. They are a form of manipulation. They are classic examples of the unresolved anger disguised in passive-aggressive behavior.

Are there people in your life whom you are not particularly fond of? Do you do things to irritate them? Sometimes our behavior is so subtle it's hard to detect, and even then, we try to make excuses for it. At the women's shelter where I work, we had a staff person whose job it was to transport the women to and from their appointments. There was one resident whom she could not stand. Granted, the woman was, well, *challenging*, to deal with.

So, the driver was consistently late picking her up for

her appointments. The resident became even more enraged, but the driver made all sorts of excuses. "I was stuck in traffic." "I had trouble with the van." There was one excuse after another. The conditions between them worsened, and I was enlisted to try to get to the bottom of it.

After some mediation, I discovered that the driver was angry with the resident because she was demanding and wanted things done exactly according to her plans. If things did not go precisely the way she wanted, she became belligerent, cursing at the driver and threatening to get her fired. Unable to convince the woman to change her attitude, the driver decided that she would teach her a lesson by making her wait.

Of course, we can all look objectively at this and realize that the driver's behavior is classic PA. By maintaining her cool, she could not outwardly be accused of being angry and deliberately irritating her passenger, yet that is clearly what she was doing.

Many who are PA are not even aware of the fact that they are angry or that their actions are hurtful to others. If you are dealing with people whom you believe fit into this category, you might want to begin with this assumption. Give them the benefit of the doubt. Instead of confronting them with hostility or accusations, ask questions.

> Are you aware that when you do or say this, that I feel ____?
> Do you realize that this affects me in this way: ____?
> And that when you do that, ____ may also happen?

Listen to, but do not dwell on, the responses to these questions. Rather, move quickly to your request. "I need you to (do or say) *this* instead." You have clearly defined the other party's unacceptable behavior and called attention to it. You have also set limits by expressing your expectations. Be strong and confident (and polite) in your mannerisms, and you should see some positive changes.

Be careful, too, of your own actions and the way you treat others. Do you call your children nicknames they don't like? Do you refuse to move over so the other car can pass you because he flashes his lights at you? Do you play mind games with your new boyfriend because your previous lover used you? Do you refrain from giving one hundred percent of yourself at your job because no one else gives one hundred percent? Then do you complain when the promotion goes to the boss's son instead of you? Do you ignore certain people and treat them as if they don't exist? Take a look at your actions. Passive-aggressive behavior will interfere with your relationships and your ability to be happy and successful.

Motive! Motive! Motive! Pay attention to what you're doing, what you're saying, and what you're not doing or saying as well. Whenever your behavior causes distress in another, or if you have any pangs of guilt or remorse, stop and ask yourself, "What is the real reason I made this choice?" And even if you don't feel guilty, ask yourself that question anyway. It will reveal a lot about who you are. And be *totally honest*.

That is extremely difficult to do because most of us live in denial. And you know what they say about denial (or at least what *I* say).

Denial is not a river in Egypt. It is a black abyss of fear
that keeps us imprisoned in false truths and obstructs
our chances of achieving personal greatness.*

(Highlight! Highlight! Highlight!)
*Janet Pfeiffer, United Nations, October 6, 2004

Only when people are completely and totally honest about
their motives can they even *begin* to be happy and successful.
Anything less is a lie, and nothing can survive on lies.

Think about how the other party feels when you treat her in
this way. Look for better ways of handling the situation. Work
on being more compassionate. Don't forget about karma. It can,
and will, turn around and bite you in the butt eventually.

Think about what kind of legacy you want to leave
behind for your children, grandchildren, the world, when
you're gone. Do you want to be remembered as someone
who caused pain and suffering to those around you? Or do
you want to be remembered as someone who was always
kind and courteous?

One of my most challenging and stimulating seminars is
entitled "To Thine Own Self Be True: A Soul-Searching Journey
of Introspection and Self-Revelation." It is based on the "eight
profound questions of self-discovery" and is a real eye-opener
for most people. Participants are challenged to face some hard
truths about themselves. It's gut-wrenching for many, but has
proven to be a liberating experience for everyone.

Here's a thought-provoking activity for those of you who
are not quite up to the challenge of "To Thine..." It's called
The Testimonial Dinner. Get out a notebook.

This is a written assignment.

Imagine that you have lived a full century. (Congratulations, you old geezer!) The President of the United States is throwing a huge gala in your honor. Everyone who has ever met or known you has been invited to attend this magnificent celebration. In lieu of gifts, each has been asked to write you a testimonial letter, recounting the relationship the two of you shared.

However, due to a shortage of time (after all, we don't know how much longer you'll be with us), only two people have the opportunity to read what they have written: the person who has most loved and admired you during your lifetime and the one who has most disliked you. You must pen both of those letters using your own imagination as to what each would have to say.

This is a tough exercise. If you can really face the truth about who you are and the way you've treated others throughout your life, you can learn a lot. And, you're being given a second chance to correct any hurtful and destructive behavior. While this activity may prove to be a bit painful, I want you to focus on how insightful and liberating it can be as well.

We have certainly covered a wide array of personalities and behaviors, all of which are basically, well, negative. That's depressing and discouraging. It seems like everything we say and do is counterproductive.

How many of you remember Johnny Carson and the Great Karnak? Ed McMahon would read the answer contained in the sealed envelope, and Johnny would give him the question. "The answer is *assertive*. The question: *What personality type and corresponding behavior are the most effective and safe when dealing with anger?*"

(Ta-da! I just did the same thing as Carson, but I don't hear anyone laughing. Not funny enough?)

I'd like to speak to you about the most beneficial and productive personality in regards to anger.

D) Assertive

The assertive individual is blessed with the gift of self-confidence, a strong belief in one's own ability to handle oneself well in any given circumstance. One who is assertive cares about the well-being of the other party and is not threatened by their differences.

On the contrary, differences are viewed as assets in the relationship. One is able and willing to take the initiative in seeking a positive outcome to the existing situation, making sure all parties are comfortable and satisfied with the results. Mutual respect for all involved is evident and provides a trusting foundation on which the relationship is built. Boundaries are set, appreciated, and enforced in order to create a healthier interaction between all those involved. This is the healthiest of the anger personalities because its basis is confidence and concern, unlike the others, which have foundations rooted in fear.

You can easily identify someone who is assertive. They have an air of strength about them, a kind of quiet confidence that emanates from their very beings. They do not yell, rant, rave, or threaten. Their tone of voice is steady and strong. Others listen when they speak. It is clear that they believe in themselves and feel strongly that they can handle the situations they are in. They are very clear as to what it is that they want and expect from each person. Natural or learned, they are leaders who take the initiative and move things forward. Always conscious of each person's needs (unmet needs = anger) and feelings, they eagerly seek to resolve any disagreements or disputes to the satisfaction of all.

Do you see the difference between aggressive and assertive? One is based on fear and threats; the other, self-confidence and concern. There's a huge difference, but many fail to see that. They believe that aggressive *is* assertive. It is not. Far from it—they are on opposite ends of the spectrum. Can any of you see yourselves as true assertives? Although you may not have entered this world as such, you can learn to develop this type of persona. I have.

While I haven't yet perfected it, I am a work in progress. I have become much more comfortable with myself and therefore am far less threatened by others (how they perceive me, what they may or may not think of me, even whether or not they like me).

I have developed many of the skills necessary to handle the most challenging of situations and have proven to myself that I am quite capable. That does not mean that things always work out according to my plans, but rather that regardless of the outcome, I can maintain my level of integrity and composure. I rarely give in to the manipulations of others. (I say "rarely" because I will admit that there have still been times when I've become weak and fallen prey to the pressure. However, it happens far less often than in years past.)

Mediators, hostage negotiators, conflict-resolution specialists, peacemakers: they all fall into this category. They have to. One sign of insecurity or the loss of one's temper, even for a split second, can have catastrophic consequences.

I would venture to say that most of them were trained in assertiveness. It didn't come naturally for all of them, yet they have mastered the art. So can you. Anyone can. Building self-confidence rests largely on referencing our past successes and using them as a foundation for future endeavors.

Take a look at anything you have had to learn to do in your life that was a challenge. Start from when you were a child. The first time you tried to ride a bike (a two-wheeler, not a tricycle), did you find yourself speeding down the sidewalk unscathed, or did you lose control, take a nose dive for the curb, and scrape both your knees and maybe an elbow or two? I don't know anyone who mastered the art of balancing on two wheels on the very first try. And yet, after several attempts, you were soon riding with the best of them.

Taking your SATs, going on your first job interview, facing life after the loss of a spouse, recovering from a serious illness—you've proven time and time again that you are far more capable than what you imagined. You have proven to yourself that you can face and overcome any of life's challenges. And not only that, you can emerge a stronger person than before. Self-confidence is the belief in one's own abilities, tapped or dormant. Acquiring the necessary skills and strategies will enhance your rate of success.

D.) Assertive Behavior

There are distinct characteristics common to assertive behavior. Typically, this behavior constitutes speaking in "I" terms. The use of the word *you* often appears threatening to the other party ("You are driving too fast" as compared to

"I'm not comfortable traveling at such high speeds"). The first statement can be interpreted as a criticism or complaint against the driver. The second speaks of the feelings of the passenger, which are non-judgmental.

In fact, assertiveness speaks of feelings and needs. "I can't hear what Grandmother's saying with all this noise (a statement of my *position*, a *fact*). I need you to sit quietly while I'm speaking with her on the phone (a *request*)." There is no blame: simply a statement of needs. Most people will respond better to this type of approach rather than an accusatory statement or demand such as, "You're making too much noise (an *opinion*)! Sit down and be quiet now (a *demand*)!"

Practice P R O D:
statement of my *position* (fact) and *request*
vs. *opinion* (perception) and *demand*.
You choose.

As logical as this may sound, you might still encounter some who will be offended by what you are saying. There are always a few who will misinterpret or refuse to understand your methods. You can only try to reassure them of your position and continue to move forward with this process. Again, you are not responsible for how others interpret your actions, and while this process is not foolproof, it does increase your chances for success.

Additionally, assertive behavior deals with facts only and states them as simply and directly as possible. There is no blame or judgment, no accusations or criticisms. "I asked you to stop at the post office on the way home from work today and pick up stamps for me. I haven't received them yet." Do you see that there were no assumptions made, no accusations? I simply stated my *request* and then my current *position*.

Now look at the accusatory method. "I told you to get me stamps, and you didn't. I knew you wouldn't remember." How do I know for certain that he didn't get them? Perhaps he did and just hasn't given them to me yet. As soon as you make an assumption or accusation, the other person goes into self-defense mode. They feel as though they are under attack and immediately begin to plan their defense. At this point, the conversation can take a drastic turn for the worse, and if immediate steps to turn things around are not taken, all attempts for an understanding can be lost.

Mutual respect for all parties is fundamental to assertiveness. Considering each person and his position as equally as valuable as everyone else's can avert the possibility that either party might become offended. This can prevent an argument from occurring or a breakdown in communication.

You've all witnessed people with these characteristics: they take the initiative in trying to resolve incidents and remain fair and open-minded throughout the process.

They are good listeners and take into consideration both sides. Seeking to uncover and understand the truth, they ask questions rather than make assumptions.

Those who seek the truth ask questions.
Those who fear the truth form assumptions or judgments.

(Another one of my brilliant quotes that needs highlighting!)

JANET PFEIFFER

Let me explain. Have you ever prematurely jumped to a conclusion about someone? My rose garden was trampled, and many of my prized bushes were seriously damaged. I decide that it must be the kids who live next door to me because they're always running through my yard even though I've told them a dozen times to stay off my property.

I'm furious, so I go storming over to their house and start screaming at their parents, making all kinds of threats to ensure that this behavior will finally stop. They assure me that it was not their boys. While it is true that they sometimes cut through my yard, they would never be so disrespectful as to damage my gardens. But I don't want to hear it. I've already made up my mind. They're guilty!

Isn't this a classic example of aggressive behavior? I'm not interested in the truth. If I were, I would ask questions and gain as much information as possible before forming an opinion. In this case, I'm more interested in finding someone to blame. I'm angry, and I need a target for my anger so these young boys will do just fine.

If I were assertive, I would have calmly gone to their house and stated what had happened. I would have asked if anyone had any information that they could share with me. If one or more of the boys had admitted fault, I would have then stated my position as to what I needed to have happen next.

Perhaps it would be that I would expect them to clean up whatever mess had been made and also pay to replace the damaged plants. Even if no one admitted any wrongdoing, I am still free to state my position, such as, "Based on what has just occurred, I need to make certain this doesn't happen again. Therefore, my property is now off-limits to all children." My focus was not on blame, but rather on finding a solution to the problem.

Have you ever been unfairly accused of something you didn't do? It doesn't feel very good, does it? In fact, it will very often ignite feelings of anger in us toward our accusers. And yet, how many times have you yourself treated others that way? You're not interested in the truth. You know what you *want* to believe, and that's all there is to it.

How often do we want to believe the worst about someone? It validates our anger and allows us to hold onto it. Imagine what would happen if you discovered the truth and realized that it was not what you thought it was? Would you no longer have a reason to be angry? For some, giving up the anger means relinquishing power (remember, anger makes us feel powerful). And sadly, there are some who are so insecure that they need their anger to feel important and strong.

Do you have children? You do? Me, too! Aren't they wonderful? Can you recall when they were toddlers and had their first tantrums? I can. I have a really good memory. My children are long past those years. Many parents subscribe to the belief that they should just let them throw the tantrums and get them out of their systems. Then when they have quieted down, they can speak to them about what's troubling them.

That was not my philosophy, not by a long shot. I had no tolerance for a screaming, out-of-control child lying on the floor kicking and thrashing about. My patience wore thin really quickly. I took my child firmly by the arm, got right up close to his face (almost nose-to-nose), looked him square in the eyes, and stated in the most controlled voice I could, "Stop. Stop it right now. Sit down and calm down *now*."

I didn't have to yell. I may have had to repeat it one or two more times, but I never had to yell, not with this, at least. (I wish I had applied this strategy to other aspects of parenting, but I didn't. Ask my kids; they'll tell you. They used to refer to me as the "Great American Scream Machine," like the roller coaster at Six Flags. It was not a term of endearment.)

Being assertive in this situation proved extremely beneficial. All my children threw only one tantrum each in their lives. They learned very quickly that screaming did not work with Mommy. When one is confident that one can handle the situation and is not threatened by the other person's behavior, an inner strength emerges and takes command of the situation.

There are times when being assertive comes easier to me than at other times. The circumstance, the individuals involved, the stakes at hand, all play an important role. I feel much more comfortable dealing with certain people than with others. In some situations there is a lot more at risk, too.

I may be perfectly comfortable asserting myself with my best friend, while I may be somewhat apprehensive with my boss. My friend may be more accepting of me and willing to hear what I have to say, while my boss may feel threatened should I approach him. My friend loves me for who I am and will always be there for me. My boss, on the other hand, has the power to fire me should he perceive me as hostile.

It is important for me to examine each situation that is causing me concern to gain a better understanding of where my insecurities lie, get to the root of the fear, and address it. If not, it will hold me back from following through and getting the best possible results.

Once again, let me reiterate that assertive behavior focuses on *solution*, not blame. Dealing with facts only, maintaining mutual respect for all parties, feeling confident and capable and focusing on needs and feelings will create a much more agreeable outcome for all. Both parties will retain their integrity and dignity, which are key factors in maintaining healthy, long-term relationships.

PART 2

PRACTICE MAKES PERFECT

GETTING THE UPR HAND ON ANGER

Thanks so much for sticking with me this far. This has been quite a learning experience, hasn't it? What was your biggest "Ah-ha" moment? Really? That's wonderful! Are you ready to take what you've learned and put it into practice? Great. Many people believe that knowledge is power. But only when one applies that knowledge does change occur.

Many people have the misconception that it's important to control your anger in certain situations. As I said earlier, it is nearly impossible (and definitely not healthy) to try to control it. Anger is much too powerful a force to control. What you need to do is learn how to *manage* it safely and effectively.

You want to be able to decide when to become angry and just how angry you need to be at that moment. (Remember

I told you that anger is a useful and necessary emotion? It's how you handle it that determines if it is a positive or negative force.) You also want to be the one who decides how and when to let go of it. You do not ever want to allow your emotions to control you. You need to get the UPR (pronounced "upper") HAND on anger:

U: understand
P: process
R: release

First, you need to *understand* what you're really dealing with and what the anger is trying to tell you. By now, you have a much deeper awareness of this. Hurt, fear, frustration, unmet needs, unrealistic expectations—remember?

Next, *process* the experience. That's why I gave you The Thirteen Quick Questions for Clarity. Use them. They work. I also gave you a comprehensive look at the *root* emotions and how to resolve each one of them. What does each one reveal about you? What are the core issues behind each of them that you need to address? Please don't miss out on doing the work now. It absolutely pays huge dividends in the long run.

Finally, *release*: once you understand the message behind the anger, focus on the solution to whatever you are upset about. You must let go of the anger in order to refocus your mind on creating a positive outcome to the situation. Your mind is only capable of experiencing one emotion at a time. Be careful what you choose to feel because your feeling will determine your behaviors and ultimately the outcome.

Wayne Dyer (one of my absolute favorite authors—I

definitely recommend you read any of his books, especially *The Power of Intention*) says that "you cannot solve a problem with the same mind that created it." By that, he means that problems only exist in the mind. (Remember the Jamaican tour guide?) You must change your perception, reframe your thoughts, get them off the problem, and onto the solution.

So whether you are someone who is aggressive, passive, or passive-aggressive, I am going to assume (I know, I'm taking a big risk here) that the reason you are reading this book is because you are unhappy with the way you have allowed your anger to manipulate and control your life, and you are now ready to take a stand and make a change. Good for you! I am very proud of you. Making change takes commitment and effort, but not only is it possible, it is *entirely worth it.*

> If you keep doing what you're doing,
> You'll keep getting what you've got.

> (Yet another highlight.)

Let's get started making some changes. Change is good, especially if we're talking about socks. It's good to change them every day... otherwise, they get nasty.

But changing the way we behave is even more beneficial. Periodically, one needs to reexamine one's life and identify what is no longer working well. In that way one can make the necessary changes for improvement. It's called *growth*. And the opposite of growth is what? Death.

Let's begin by talking about boundaries. Most of us are pretty familiar with that term by now. It's been around for a long time. However, I think it is important to clearly define exactly what it is so we're at least all on the same page. (I have *no* idea what page I'm on. Do you?)

Boundaries: the rules and regulations of relationship, the guidelines we set up that determine how we want to be treated as well as what we find to be offensive and unacceptable.

All healthy relationships are founded on this principle. Any partnership that has sustained longevity understands this concept. There is a mutual respect for each individual's preference as to how he wants to be treated. Each person has the right to decide for himself exactly how he wants others to interact with him. What one party finds perfectly acceptable, another may find highly offensive. But each viewpoint has value and must be honored.

Boundaries are not about control. They are designed to enhance and strengthen the relationship. Do you know what the single most deciding factor is in determining the success of any relationship? It's how well both parties are getting their needs met. And we all know what happens if needs are being denied. Anger surfaces, and anger can lead to fighting, resentment, revenge, etc. That spells disaster for any couple. Therefore, it is critical that both sides make sure from the get-go (no, not that cute little lizard that sells car insurance) that their needs are being acknowledged, validated, and fulfilled.

But how can one be assured of that if the other person doesn't clearly understand what the first party needs? This is where boundaries and assertiveness come into play: boundaries state with certainty and clarity exactly what is expected from both sides. Let me give you an example.

I am a non-smoker, and while I do believe that people

have a right to smoke if they want, I have absolutely no desire to be subjected to secondhand smoke, for a variety of reasons, mostly health-related.

So what did I do? I married a smoker. How brilliant was that? (He's a really nice guy, though. What can I say?) While I am not happy at all about his *choice* to smoke, I do respect his *right* to do so. When we began dating, I needed to let him know up front how I felt and what I needed from him regarding this issue. I explained to him that if he felt compelled to smoke, he needed to do so away from me. I did not want to see him smoke (it is very upsetting for me to see someone I love engaging in self-destructive behavior), nor did I want to smell it.

Again, secondhand smoke is harmful to my health as well as the fact that to a non-smoker, it smells really bad. He has respected my request, so it has never created a problem between us. Had I not addressed this early on, it could have been a deal-breaker in our relationship.

There are several things to take notice of in this case: first, I spoke up early and expressed clearly how I felt and what I needed from him. Second, I did not criticize or berate him because of his habit. Also, he respected my request and has always honored it. These points are key factors in determining how effective boundaries will be for both parties; early establishment of the guidelines presented in a respectful manner plus the other party's willingness to comply will yield positive results.

Let me clarify the difference between boundaries and control. Boundaries are founded on the desire to create and sustain a mutually satisfying partnership for both sides. They encompass the elements of concern and support, making sure everyone is satisfied and comfortable. They are fair and reasonable, taking into account how the needs and wants of each side may possibly impact the other.

Cooperation and compromise are important components and are utilized whenever necessary, without sacrificing the integrity of either side. Boundaries are meant to enhance and create balance, to protect and support, to encourage and respect. Does this sound remotely similar to assertiveness? You bet it does! One who sets and enforces boundaries is confident, self-loving, and cares about the other person's well-being as well.

Control, on the other hand, is based on fear. There is no concern for the other person. The controller only cares about himself and making sure everything goes his way. Here's an example:

Your wife decides to become a vegan: no meat, no dairy. "This is a much healthier way of eating," she declares, as she cleans out the refrigerator. "Say goodbye to the Swiss cheese and eggs, too!"

"But I'm a meat and potatoes guy," you remind her. "I want my sirloin."

"Too bad, honey. This is much better for you. You'll see in the long run."

Is her behavior based on mutual concern for *your* needs as well as hers? She'll tell you it is. She's only doing this because she loves you and it is a much healthier way of eating. You should appreciate what she's doing. What she is neglecting to see is that your needs are equally as important as hers, yet she is completely disregarding them. (Your unmet needs may turn to anger.) And on top of that, she is imposing guilt on you for failing to appreciate her selfless actions.

Clearly, this is about control, not concern. Her "boundaries" declare that there will no longer be meat or meat products in the house. Her needs are completely overshadowing yours. She has a right to decide for herself what she chooses to consume. She does not have a right to impose her choices on you.

Too often, we confuse control with boundaries and vice versa. The request that we make of the other party must be fair and reasonable as well as flexible whenever necessary.

Be aware of control. Refer back to aggressive and explosive behavior as well as passive-aggressive. If the limits one is inflicting on you contradict your values, disregard your feelings and needs, make you feel uncomfortable or unimportant, are outrageous and unfair, or impose guilt or shame upon you, please reconsider your relationship. This is not healthy for you.

Healthy relationships should feel safe, comfortable, secure, and nurturing. Settle for anything less, and you are cheating yourself. In the long run, chances are slim to nil that it will survive the test of time.

Understanding what boundaries are and the importance of having them is only a third of the lesson. Along with your right to set your own limits, may I add that each person is entitled to write his own set of rules as well? Just as you expect that others respect you, you must also be willing to respect others' guidelines, however different from yours.

Writing your rules is great, but how is the other person supposed to know how you want to be treated? Unless you are with the amazing Kreskin, chances are you'll have to explain those rules. People are not mind readers. Let each person know early on exactly how you expect to be treated. After all…

We teach people how to treat us.

(You know the routine.)

I am not suggesting that the moment you meet someone, you immediately blurt out your boundaries. "Hello, my name is Janet. It's such a pleasure to meet you. I don't allow cursing, tardiness, or racial jokes. You must always be on time, speak to me politely, and send me thank you notes for the gifts I give you." Imagine how many people would look at me as though I were insane and quickly remove themselves from my presence?

What I am suggesting is that as the friendship progresses, subtle comments can be made that inform the other as to the way you prefer to be treated. "I used to date a guy who was always late. It really annoyed me, and as many times as I asked him to be on time, he kept ignoring my requests. Needless to say, we are no longer together." Or, I may be bold and state exactly what I need. "I hate being late. Except for extraordinary circumstances, I expect people to be punctual."

Additionally, when a situation arises that does not please me, it is important for me to address it immediately, or soon thereafter. To neglect doing so is to give the other permission to repeat it. If I tell my students to refer to me as "Miss Pfeiffer," but they call me "Miss Janet" instead, and I don't correct it at that moment, then in essence I am giving them permission to continue. Each time they call me "Miss Janet" instead of what I had requested, it creates resentment inside me, and that can easily convert to full-blown anger.

Sometimes we may find it necessary to repeat and reinforce what we expect. It is often helpful to begin by asking a question: "Sharon, do you realize that whenever we disagree on something, you tell me I'm wrong for feeling the way I do?" (Not everyone pays attention to their behavior.) "Why do you do that?" (This gives me the opportunity to understand her motive. Remember, "Those who seek the truth ask questions.") "When that happens, I feel embarrassed and unimportant. Please don't do that again" (feelings, then position). "If you do, I will not respond to you, but rather walk away in silence, and I would prefer not to have to do that" (reasonable consequences).

Let me add, too, that you must be specific and detailed about your rules. If I tell my boss that I expect to be treated with the same dignity as my colleagues, but he refers to me as "honey" and I then become offended, was I specific enough in my request? I need to let him know exactly what treatment works for me and what doesn't.

"Mr. Miller, as an associate in your firm, I feel it is imperative that I be in attendance for all board meetings; am afforded the same company privileges as my colleagues, including salary; and be addressed as Mr. Donaldson as well. This will ensure a professional and mutually satisfying partnership for both of us. Thank you for your understanding in this matter."

The sooner one establishes and conveys her guidelines to others, the easier things move forward. The longer you wait, the more difficult it becomes. Humans are creatures of habit and are for the most part uncomfortable with change. When someone tries to initiate change, he is often met with resistance. The other may pout, whine, complain, or threaten in an attempt to revert things back to the way they were. This is that person's comfort zone, but it may not be yours. And while his position must be considered valid (it is to him), it needs to be negotiated to the point where both sides are comfortable with the outcome. Too often, one side resorts to manipulation as a form of trying to revert things back to the old pattern.

When I was with my abuser, I had begun to learn about boundaries in the anger management workshop I was participating in. Our assignment for the week was to set some boundaries with someone we were having difficulty with. (Hmm, that's a tough one. Whom could I pick?) I approached him and told him that I was tired of him hitting me (my feeling) and that it needed to stop (my position).

As is typical with an aggressor, he felt he was losing control and needed to regain it as quickly as possible. He resorted to manipulation. I will never forget his words. "I don't know what's happened to you," he said. "But you *used to* be nice!"

"No," I replied. "I used to be a wimp. I'm not afraid of you anymore." I stood my ground, determined to initiate some much-needed change and to be treated with the respect that I deserved.

Since he was an abuser (this also occurs with one who has become much too comfortable with the way things are), he was unwilling to accommodate my requests. The fear of losing control ultimately led to the demise of the relationship. *Lucky for you*, you're probably thinking. Yes and no. It's sad to think that my simple request, which would have made the relationship so much safer and happier for both of us, went unfulfilled and two people in love had to say goodbye forever.

Okay, so the first step is the creation of the boundaries. The second is to state them to the other party. Third, and this is critical for its success, is enforcement. There must be swift and reasonable consequences for those who choose to disregard our requests.

CREATE >STATE > ENFORCE

If I tell you, when we're on the phone and we get into a disagreement, that I do not like it when you slam the phone down on me and yet you continue to do it, are my boundaries effective? Absolutely not. They are, in essence, a joke. Why would anyone make the effort to change a behavior I find unacceptable if there isn't a price to pay?

I like to use the analogy of the speed limits on our roadways. Imagine that you're traveling on the Garden State Parkway doing seventy-five in a fifty-five-mph zone. A police officer pulls you over.

"License and registration."

"What seems to be the problem, Officer?"

"Do you know that you were traveling twenty miles per hour over the allowed speed limit?"

"Oh, gee, I'm sorry. I promise I won't do it again."

Now, imagine what would happen if the police officer said, "Oh, well, as long as you understand that you were in violation of the law, I'll overlook it. Just make sure it doesn't happen again."

Right. How many of us would be more obedient of the law

next time? I'm guessing not too many. Why should we? There are absolutely no consequences for our actions. Consequences make us think twice. I'd rather pay attention to my behavior initially than to have to pay the price in fines. And the price has to be significant—reasonable but significant.

If the officer wrote me a summons for $1.95, do you think I'd learn? Two bucks? No big deal! But a $70 ticket, plus a $200 surcharge on my insurance each year for the next three years, and throw in some points on my license for good measure, and well, that's a different story. That hurts! Trust me; we all learn better when the price we pay for breaking the law (civil or personal) is significant. Keep in mind though, that it needs to be fair and reasonable.

I told my abuser that the next time he put his hands on me I was going to call the police and have him arrested. I was serious. He didn't think I was. Sure enough, the next time he hit me, I dialed 911 and had him arrested. He was furious, but I had to teach him that I meant what I said and that I would not back down. To do so would have guaranteed the continuation of the abuse. If he wanted to be with me, he needed to have enough respect for me to treat me in a way I approved of. I was no longer willing to suffer at the hands of someone who claimed to love me.

While the purpose of boundaries is to create and promote healthy relationships and improve the quality of them for both parties, sadly that is not always the case. Some people will choose to disregard your needs. They may argue and fight with you. They may choose to ignore you or try to make you feel selfish. Some may even decide to leave.

As sad as that may be, my feeling is that if you truly care

JANET PFEIFFER

about me, you would be willing to give me only what is the best for me. To withhold that is a blatant statement of disregard for me. That is not concern, and I do not need to fill my life with people who do not care about my well-being. There are over six billion people in this world. If you do not care about me, *truly* care about me, there are potentially 5,999,999,999 others who will.

Setting and enforcing boundaries is risky, but well worth it. You will weed out those who are selfish, self-centered, and arrogant and fill your life with loving, caring, supportive people.

Let me round off this chapter by encouraging you to:

Practice the 3 Ps
Plan how you want to be treated.
Practice how you're going to express that to others.
(Rehearse, rehearse, rehearse!)
Persist: be firm, don't give in.
Expect Respect.

DIF-"FUSE"—
DON'T
DETONATE!

Previously, I spoke about a very destructive method of dealing with anger: explosive/aggressive. One who yells, threatens, hits, punches walls, or throws a tantrum is acting out in a negative and counterproductive way. (I know. It's not you. It's your friend. I remember.)

Let me share with you (to share with your friend) a technique I've developed and used that has helped thousands of people who have this same condition. Let me start by asking you what you would do if your clothes caught on fire? Do you remember what Fireman Mac told you when he visited your fourth-grade class? (Fireman Mac is my husband. Do you remember him: tall, skinny guy with red hair and a mustache? No? Maybe you were absent that day.)

Let me refresh your memory—and don't forget this. It could save your life someday. If your clothes were to catch on fire, you would stop, drop, and roll, right? And the reason for this is … That's right; you want to put out the fire as quickly as possible before it harms you. Although fire itself is not bad, if it's misused or gets out of control, it can cause severe pain and suffering, possibly even death. So you need something that is easy to remember, easy to apply, and highly effective. This technique most definitely is.

As I mentioned earlier, anger is not a bad emotion. It's how we choose to use it that determines whether it becomes a positive or negative force. Anger, when properly managed, can be a motivating force that brings about positive change. Anger, mismanaged or out of control, can be a highly destructive and sometimes deadly force.

Therefore, it is imperative that we learn a method of calming down as quickly as possible to minimize any potential threat. Next, we want to be able to manage it in the most effective way possible and channel it for the most good.

I don't remember how, but I came up with a brilliant idea as to how to accomplish this. (I know, sometimes I'm so smart, I even amaze myself!) It's actually a derivative of the stop, drop, and roll. So, the next time your "friend" gets angry, tell her Janet said to:

Stop, walk, and talk.

(Don't forget to highlight.)

JANET PFEIFFER

See how easy that is? Three simple words, easy to remember, easy to use, yet powerful in results. Let me explain how this works.

Step 1: Stop

Suppose you're working on a project and nothing is going right. No matter what you try, you run into an obstacle. You find yourself getting frustrated (root of anger) and losing patience.

You feel as though you're going to explode. You just want to take this project, throw it in the trash, and forget the whole thing. But you know that is not really a smart thing to do. You need to complete this task, but you are at your wit's end. (Try going back to the beginning of your wit and see if that helps. It might.)

In any event, at that moment of frustration, I want you to stop; stop whatever you're doing. As soon as you do so, you will immediately prohibit your frustration from increasing. You know from past experience that if you continue to work, you will continue to become more and more agitated. And the higher your level of anxiety, the lower your lever of competency. So, just stop.

Step 2: Walk

Next, I want you to walk away. Just get away from the task for a few minutes (or longer, if necessary). You know that old adage "out of sight, out of mind"? Here is a perfect example of how and where it works. When you walk away, you remove yourself from the trigger (not the source, though, which is frustration or fear). Once away from it, you can now refocus your thoughts and gain some clarity. This is a perfect opportunity to take a few moments, breathe deeply, chill out, and regroup. Give yourself enough time to calm yourself down. If you don't, your emotions will continue to escalate, and the situation will only worsen.

Let me mention here that as we go through life, we respond to every occurrence in one of two ways: either on an emotional level or an intellectual level. Something happens; we witness an event. Sometimes we get emotional about it and respond accordingly. Other times we think about it before making a decision as to what we're going to do next.

Here's an example: You have not been doing well financially. Bills have been piling up, and credit card debt is getting deeper. One day you receive a notice in the mail that your home has gone into foreclosure. You throw your hands up in despair and declare that you have had enough. There is no way out. You decide to file for bankruptcy. You are so filled with hopelessness and fear that you base your decision on an avalanche of emotions. This is not the best time to be making a decision of such magnitude that will undoubtedly have a serious impact on your life for years to come.

Before making such a life-altering decision, it would be wise to put the notice of foreclosure down, walk away from it, and give yourself time to calm down and sort through your feelings for a while. Even if it takes you several days or a week, make sure that your emotions are back in check before taking action. Once your emotions have subsided, your intellectual brain takes over. Your brain gathers information, collects data, sorts it out, rationalizes, explores all possible options, and weighs each potential outcome before making a decision. The final determination is based on reason and intelligent choice rather than emotion. I have consistently found that intellect works infinitely better than emotion.

Step 3: Talk

The third phase of this process is to talk out what's bothering you with a third party, preferably someone who's trustworthy and objective. Call a friend, visit your therapist, drop in to see your pastor: whoever you feel is a good listener and will offer some valuable insights as well as a few words of encouragement, talk to them.

Explain what is going on, what you're trying to accomplish, and how frustrated you're becoming. Be very clear as to what your main objective is: what is your primary goal? Fill them in on as many of the details about what is not working out as planned. Ask them if they've ever been in a situation similar to yours and how they handled it. What steps did they take? Can they offer any guidance? Is there anything you are doing wrong, anything you need to correct or do differently? Can they offer some physical assistance, or do they know of anyone who can?

Listen to and seriously consider their advice. Even if the other party has never been in the exact situation you are at that moment, can they offer some suggestions as to how to handle frustration in general?

"Well, there's no one I can talk to that I trust," you complain. Then talk to yourself. You are incredibly intelligent, and you already know the answers to most of life's questions anyway. Refer back to the chapter where we talked about frustration. Reread the questions I gave you to clarify frustration, and answer them. You'll gain a lot of insight that will help you to put things into perspective.

And what about God? What about talking to him? He is always available, willing, and surprisingly *has* all of the answers you're looking for. "That's fine, except I've tried that, and it doesn't work. He doesn't answer me." Ah, yes, he does. Always. It may just not be in the way you expect. We don't necessarily hear words as we do when a human answers us. Many times it comes in the form of a feeling, a sense, an awareness. It's subtle. It may be a sign. Sometimes he speaks to us through others.

Then, too, it may not always be the answer we're looking for, and so we may ignore it. If you ask, *listen*—even if it's not the answer you wanted to hear. Accept that his answers are *always* the right ones.

Assuming that you've taken my advice here (oh, I almost forgot, this isn't for you.): assuming that your *friend* has followed my advice, the next step is to go back and try once again to complete the project.

Stop, walk, and talk gives the individual the opportunity to take a much-needed break, calm down, think things through carefully and thoroughly. In addition, they will gain a deeper understanding and perhaps a new perspective and hopefully come up with a new game plan to make things work out. Emotions are in check, and intellect is in charge. If the frustration begins to surface again, repeat the process. Most projects are not a matter of life or death and can be completed at a later date.

This same process can be used when having a conversation with another person. You start out fine, but somewhere along the way, things take a turn for the worse. You disagree on an important point, and feelings begin to escalate. Try as you will, you just can't seem to get the other person to agree with you—even though you know for a fact that you're right. Right?

You find yourself losing patience. Anger is on the verge of showing its ugly face, and you begin formulating in your mind a nasty commentary. Before you erupt and say something that cannot be bleeped out, apply the stop, walk, and talk technique. Stop talking, walk away, and talk things over with someone else until you've calmed down. When you've given yourself enough time to rethink carefully how you're going to proceed, then return and complete the process. Repeat if necessary.

"Well, that all sounds well and good, Janet," you say. "But the reality of it is that it is not always possible just to get up and leave."

"Sure it is."

One woman who attended one of my seminars said that if she was in an important business meeting and her boss began to aggravate her, there was no way she could just get up and walk out.

"Tell him that you have to go to the bathroom," I suggested. "No one's going to deny you that, especially if you tell them you have to go *really badly*."

She looked at me kind of strangely.

"And being a woman, you can stay in there for twenty minutes, *at least*. Long line."

She smiled and let out a chuckle. "Hmm, maybe you've got something there," she said.

Well, yeah, they don't call me an expert on this stuff for nothing!

Many years before I actually developed this process, I had already begun practicing it on a regular basis without fully realizing what I was doing. As I mentioned before, I had four small children when I was in my twenties and had been ill-prepared for the challenges of motherhood. Frustration was my daily companion, much to the dismay of my family. There were times when I literally felt as though I were going to explode—*physically explode*—into pieces.

My husband traveled a lot in those early years, and we were not living near family. I didn't know my neighbors very well and didn't feel as though there was anyone who could help alleviate some of my stress. I felt overwhelmed with the responsibility of "single" parenting and tried to deal with everything on my own.

But as time passed, it became more and more apparent that I was not handling things well. I was totally stressed and out of control. Little things set me off, and once I went into a rage, I couldn't stop. You've heard that term *blind rage*? It's a dark and terrifying place to be. I was hurting, but even worse, I was hurting my children. I had to do something quickly before I did some serious damage.

So I tapped into my creative brain and came up with a strategy that worked wonders. It was in essence the precursor (no, not the swearing that came first...although I did do a lot of that in those days) to the stop, walk, and talk that would follow years later.

But before I tell you my story, I need you to promise me that you won't tell anyone what I'm about to share with you. Not too many people know this about me. (I feel a little embarrassed.) Promise? Thanks.

There were plenty of times when my children, just being normal kids, would get on my nerves. That was then. Now I know better. I was doing it to myself. After all, life is a do-it-yourself project. I would find myself rapidly approaching that dark and dangerous place called rage. Not wanting to harm my children, but also knowing it was not safe for me to leave while I calmed myself down (my children were much too young to leave unattended), I instructed my children to retreat quickly to the family room, down a few steps off the kitchen. They were to close the door behind them and stay there until I told them it was safe to come back upstairs. The family room contained all their toys and a TV, so they could easily and safely entertain themselves while Mommy tended to her issues.

In my dining room, there was a closet where I kept my Electrolux canister vacuum and my eight-track player. Music is one of the most important things in my life, and I had quite an extensive collection. John Denver was by far my favorite at the time. In my opinion, he was a brilliant singer/songwriter who tragically died long before his time. He sang of the beauty and wonder of nature—another one of my most favorite things in life—and love. His music had the ability to transport me to spectacular places and calm and soothe me like no other.

I withdrew into my sanctuary, sat down on the canister vacuum, and popped in a tape. I gently pulled the door to within a few inches of being closed and let his music "fill up my senses" (that's a line from "Annie's Song"). Gradually, the lyrics and melodies washed over me and refreshed my soul. The longer I stayed, the more the stress was replaced with serenity. It didn't matter how long it took. It only mattered that I let go of all of the frustration and regained my composure.

My children were safe: safe from me and safe within the walls of our home. It could take anywhere from fifteen minutes to two hours, depending on how stressed I was at the moment. I remember one time, while sitting on my vacuum, I heard my children sneaking up the stairs. The kitchen door creaked open. There was silence for a moment. Then I heard someone whisper, "Shh, she's still in there. We'd better go back down." They knew. They gave me my space. Thank God. If they hadn't and *I* hadn't, I don't know what could have happened. But I do know that it would have been tragic.

Be creative. Your sanity, health, and well-being, as well as the safety of those around you, depend on it. This process works. It may be an inconvenience at times, but I can promise you this: in the long run, it saves time and suffering, not to mention health and relationships.

How to Soothe the Rough, Tough, and Gruff

Do you know what to do when confronted with a hostile or aggressive individual?

Run! (Just kidding.) Although ... if there is any *real* danger, you might want to consider removing yourself as quickly as possible from the source. Don't stay around and try to prove how tough you are. Your number-one priority is to keep yourself safe and free from all harm *at all times*.

Before getting started, it would serve you well to determine who the hostile person really is. Look in a mirror. Recognize yourself? *Be honest.* If you are the difficult one who is angry and aggressive, you need to acknowledge that. Dr. Phil says that you can't fix what you don't acknowledge. There's no shame in being angry. But there is weakness in not owning up to it. Next, make the decision to take some time and examine your issues. Get a grip. Put things into perspective. Calm down.

So, after careful examination, it has been properly determined that the aggressive person is not the one reading these words. I never had a moment's doubt. It's the other guy's fault, just as we suspected. (Did you catch that? I placed blame. I was just checking to see if you were paying attention.) There is no blame, only perception. Is yours accurate? If not, make the necessary adjustments now, before we go any further, okay?

All right, so you now find yourself face to face with someone who is angry, belligerent, or out of control. You have decided to stay and deal with it. Let me share with you some key points of what works and what doesn't. Assuming that you want to achieve the best possible outcome to this situation (that is a safe assumption, is it not?), the first thing you need to do is check your attitude. Refer back to the chapter on attitudes and their importance and how to choose the one that will work best for both of you.

Next, I want you to practice the R/D/C Method, three profound steps that will significantly lessen the chances of the situation escalating.

R/D/C: Refuse, Diffuse, and Choose.

Refuse

Make a conscious decision that you will not initiate or participate in negative behavior. Set and maintain your own personal standard of excellence. By that I mean, don't ever allow another person's bad behavior to change who you are. You need to decide for yourself what kind of person you want to be and then never allow another to deter you from attaining that. If you are someone who considers yourself a respectful individual, then regardless of how the other is treating you at that moment, you must still remain a respectful person.

"Are you kidding me?" you ask. "You expect me to treat someone with respect when they are disrespecting me? You're nuts!"

Well, no, yes, and no I'm not.

Let me explain. Do you admire disrespectful behavior? Most people don't. I know I don't. If you don't admire a particular quality in someone, why would you emulate it? It doesn't make sense. You become what you don't like; who you are changes, dependent upon your circumstances, who you're with, and what is going on. How smart is that? Not very, in my book (and this *is* my book, so don't forget it).

> Never allow another's bad behavior to change who you are.

(That's a highlight, folks, and a good one, too.)

Stay true to yourself. There are too many outside forces putting pressure on us to be something or someone other than what or who we really are. Set and maintain your own personal standards of excellence. Let others aspire to be like you. Be the role model for others to follow. Just *be*.

Be the example.

Just for argument's sake, let's say you fall into the trap of the other person's anger, fury, hurtfulness, etc., and respond to her in the same way she is treating you. What do you think will happen? If she's yelling at you and you shout back, do you think that she will suddenly calm down? It's highly unlikely. More often than not, it will turn into a shouting match and may turn ugly. Words become knives and cut away at our hearts. The aftermath is hurt feelings, damaged relationships, bad reputations, and regret for behaving badly.

I cannot control how the other party is acting, but I am certainly in control of how I handle myself. At the end of the day, I want to feel good about myself and the choices I made. I have to be pleased with who I am and the way I've spent my day. But more importantly, I want to know that *God* is pleased with me. In every difficult situation I find myself in, with every challenging person I encounter throughout the day, I continually turn to God for guidance. I ask him, "How do you want me to respond to or treat this person?"

And, not surprisingly, the answer is always the same: "With kindness and respect."

I am a kind person. That means that regardless of how the other person is acting, I need to remain authentic to myself and continue to be a caring and loving person. That does not mean, however, that I must allow others to mistreat me, nor does it mean that I must remain in the presence of a hurtful person and deal with bad behavior. We talked about boundaries in the last chapter. Set some and enforce them, in a manner that is consistent with who you are.

Diffuse

Learn the skills for diffusing a potentially dangerous situation. There are choices you can make that will definitely calm things down and some that will make matters worse. Be careful not to throw gasoline on the fire. Certain choices of words, gestures, facial expressions, and the like can cause things to escalate.

Have you ever witnessed someone behaving badly, and the first words out of your mouth were, "What's *your* problem?" It's so obvious that you're not inquiring out of genuine concern for them, but that it's rather an expression of disgust, annoyance, disapproval, and such.

We've all had others speak to us in that manner. How did it feel? How did you respond? "Thank you so much for asking. Actually, I am quite distressed about something. I'd like to tell you about it." I don't think so. We don't like the tone in their voice or the insinuation that there is something wrong with *us*, and so we usually offer a defensive response. "Me? *You're* the one with the problem!"

Avoid making those kinds of "fuel-injected" statements or comments. Refrain from judgments, threats, or hurtful remarks of any kind. Practice the kinds of behaviors and verbiage that calms and comforts, such as, "Let's take things down a notch. Why don't we sit down and discuss this calmly?"

Or, "I can see that you're upset. I'd like to help. Is there anything I can do?" If you use this kind of approach, you must be absolutely certain that you really do care about the individuals and what they are going through. Insincerity is easily detectable.

Sometimes humor can be an effective method of diffusion. It alleviates the tension, eases stress, puts things into perspective, and is a universal language that most can relate to. Victor Borge said, "Laughter is the shortest distance between two people." It bridges the gap. It feels good, too. And did you know that it is not humanly possible to be angry and laugh at the same time? Even the simple act of smiling renders anger powerless. Try this. The next time someone pushes your buttons, smile as you respond. I know it sounds silly, but do it anyway. See what happens. You will have a completely different reaction to the comments.

Let me caution you about one thing. Be very careful about how and when you use humor. If you don't know what you're doing, it can backfire. Be very careful never to use humor to embarrass or humiliate the other party. This is actually not humor at all, but rather passive-aggressive anger. Also, you need to know the person well enough to understand his style and level of humor. What one person finds funny, another may feel is offensive. Humor doesn't have to be roll-on-the-floor, side-splitting-laughter kind of funny. It can be subtle, silly, playful, or childish.

My husband is one of the most polite and courteous drivers I've ever known. He is a defensive driver, has really sharp reflexes, and totally obeys all traffic laws. (As odd as this may sound, it's true, my friends. He's a near-perfect driver.) His one shortcoming, however, is that he has zero tolerance for inconsiderate and ignorant drivers. He is easily irritated when driving and becomes verbally irate.

Fortunately, he never acts out his anger physically or directs it at me. However, I find it very unpleasant to be in the car with him when he goes on one of his verbal tirades. I have tried to rationalize with him and help him calm down, but he is not receptive to my suggestions. (Gee, how odd that a husband wouldn't consider what his wife is suggesting.)

Knowing him as well as I do, I know what *does* work with him. Humor: silly, third-grade, pie-in-the-face humor. (Okay, I haven't actually hit him in the face with lemon meringue … yet.) However, I have used humor with him and have found that it works quite well. Want to know what I do? I sing. *But, how is that funny?* you wonder. No, it's not my *voice* that's funny (I don't think). It's what I *sing* that is.

Actually, I wrote a song about anger that is guaranteed to make you laugh. I'll give you the lyrics—no extra charge. The melody is a well-known Christmas carol—you'll recognize it I'm sure.

"Let It Go"
By me, Janet Pfeiffer

Oh, this anger inside is frightening.
It feels like thunder and lightning.
My friends all tell me, "you know,
Let it go, let it go, let it go."

But when I'm finally in bed at night
How I want to continue this fight.
'Cause I know in my heart *I'm right!*
I clench my fists till my knuckles turn white!

But do I want to be right or happy?
Cause I'm feeling really crappy.
So I decide that it's up I will grow.
I'll let it go, let it go, let it go.
(One more time)

I'll let it go, let it go, let it go.

(Ba-rump-bump! Make that sound like a drum roll.)

Give yourselves a big round of applause and a
standing ovation!

So, how does that diffuse the tense conditions in the car with my husband? I'll just start singing in a light-hearted and silly manner. He hates this song and begs me to stop. Of course I won't until we've negotiated a deal (conflict resolution—my next book). So he tells me he'll stop being angry and complaining if I'll stop singing. Problem solved. It's a win-win for both of us. Works like a charm every time!

And while this tactic works well with *him*, I don't think it would be entirely appropriate if I were dealing with the angry driver whose car I just rear-ended because I was busy yapping on my cell phone instead of paying attention to where I was going.

Humor works great with kids, too. I remember one time when my son was little, he was trying to get two pieces of his toy to link together. It wasn't working, and he was getting quite frustrated. He began to have a fit and threw his toy down on the ground and started crying. Rather than yell at him to stop acting like a baby and pick it up, I picked up one of the pieces and imitated him. I threw it on the ground and started crying as well. He immediately stopped and looked at me with the most puzzled expression on his face. I looked back. "Well, you seemed to be having such a good time, I thought I'd try it, too."

His outburst stopped momentarily, giving me just enough time to interject a question. "What's wrong? Is there something you need? If you tell me calmly, maybe I can help." Bingo! We have a winner!

Choose

This is the final step in this process. Choose smarter, safer, and more effective methods of dealing with this type of situation than you have in the past. If you keep reacting the way you have previously, you'll always get the same results. Try something new. Let a combination of safety and fairness be the compass that directs your course of action.

Before responding, ask yourself, "If I say or do _____, then how might the other party feel or react? Is that what I really want to see happen? Am I being fair and just? Is this the best choice I can make? What are the real reasons I would say or do that? How will this choice affect me and others now and in the future?"

Think beyond the moment. Look at the long-term and far-reaching effects your choice may have on yourself and those around you. The Cherokee Indians have a deeply profound philosophy that we all need to take to heart: before doing anything, think of how it will affect seven generations to come. *Seven generations*! Most of us don't even think of ten minutes from now. Remember:

One bad choice can change your life forever.

(Highlight)

If I'm dealing with someone who is irate and I take offense and respond with a sarcastic comeback or by getting in his face, the consequences could be disastrous. How do I know that this person is not mentally unstable, or that he does not have a weapon? It is not worth taking any foolish chances. I need to care more about my safety than about proving myself.

Many years ago, I was in a restaurant having dinner with a friend. There were several young people by the bar socializing together. One of the young women left to go to the ladies' room. As she passed by another table occupied by two men about her own age, one of them stopped her, and they began to talk. Since they weren't far from where I was sitting, I could easily overhear their conversation.

It was apparent that they had dated in the past. He wanted to continue to see her, and she was clearly not interested. He would not take no for an answer. He began to pressure her, and she was becoming upset. One of her male friends from the bar walked over.

"What's the problem?" he asked the young woman.

"This guy won't leave me alone," she replied.

"The lady wants you to stop bothering her." He stood tall and spoke with confidence.

The man at the table became agitated. "I can say whatever I want to her!" he asserted.

Again, the young man replied, "I said, 'Leave her alone.'" He looked directly into the other man's eyes, obviously not intimidated by his size.

The man stood up. "You want to take this outside?" he asked in a threatening tone.

"We're not taking anything anywhere. We're done here."

He took his friend by her hand and escorted her back to the bar. The other man sat down quietly in his chair.

A situation that could have turned ugly was averted by a confident young man, not interested in impressing his peers, but whose only concern was the safety and well-being of his female companion. That's confidence. That's respect. That's maturity. That is intelligence at its best.

Too often, our egos get in the way of making smart choices. We feel disrespected and embarrassed. Our egos have been wounded, and we prepare to restore our dignity. "How dare you speak to me that way! I'll teach you!" We move into defense mode. But remember: others' bad behavior is not about you. It is an expression of whatever they are struggling with at the moment. Do not allow their problems to become your problems. I think we need to do a highlight on this one as well.

> Never allow someone else's problem
> to become your problem.

You can make matters worse by taking things personally (beware of those "to me's"). Or, you can remain detached and neutral. You can choose to respond with intellect rather than emotion. What kind of outcome would you expect to achieve by letting your brain lead instead of your feelings?

Be aware of pride as well as ego. We are far too concerned with how others will perceive us and what they will think about us if we let other people *get away* with things. Get away with what? Acting foolishly? Being out of control? Displaying poor judgment? Being insecure and immature?

I am not suggesting that you let others mistreat you and just stand there and take whatever they dish out. No, no, no! I am suggesting that you rise above the behavior and maintain your level of integrity. Choose to be the bigger person. Care less about what others think of you. Care more about God's opinion. That's really all that matters. You can choose to be part of the problem or part of the solution. But the choice *is* yours.

> Always maintain your personal level of integrity
> and dignity.
> Be authentic to who you really are.
> God's opinion of you is all that really matters.

(Highlight all three of these. They're keepers.)

Imagine what might have happened had that young man been concerned about what his friends at the bar thought of him. *Gosh, if I don't take him up on his challenge to go outside and fight, they're going to think I'm a coward.* He could have given in and gone outside to fight. And I can guarantee you that someone would have gotten hurt, maybe seriously, maybe fatally.

As a mother, I will tell you that I would rather have a son who walks away and is thought a coward but remains safe, than to have a broken, battered, or dead son who had to prove himself. Where's the glory and honor in that?

And you know what is really ironic? We humans are supposed to be the highest form of intelligent life on the planet, yet we are the only ones who are ignorant enough to fall into the trap of an intimidator. We take the bait and get hooked every time. That's excusable for a fish. It doesn't have the power to rationalize. But what's our excuse: ego and pride? There is no room for either when dealing with a threatening person in a potentially dangerous situation.

Joel Osteen, pastor of the Lakewood Church in Houston and best-selling author (*Your Best Life Now*), has his own television show. Here in New Jersey, it's on Sunday nights at six thirty. I love to listen to Joel speak. He is so genuine and has great common sense. He spoke one evening about the eagle and the crow.

Crows can be annoying birds, and sometimes when they're on the ground, they try really hard to irritate the eagle. An eagle is far larger in size than a crow and could easily put it in its place. But it doesn't. Instead, when the crow begins to bother the eagle, the eagle spreads its wings and flies away. The eagle soars to great heights far beyond the reach of the pesky crow.

Hmm, bird…human. Which possesses more intelligence, or perhaps, less ego? Either way, why not let the eagle be an example to follow. Just walk away. After all, you have absolutely nothing to lose, and everything to gain.

Recently, one of my clients who resides at the battered women's shelter relayed a story to me about a recent incident she had with another resident. Many of the women at the shelter are highly volatile and eager to find an excuse to fight. My client, "G," walked into the kitchen one afternoon to get something to eat. Immediately, one of the other mothers rushed up to her, got in her face, and began accusing G's child of hitting her son.

G could have responded defensively. After all, this was about her child. She could have become irate, demanding, or threatening herself. But no. She looked directly at the mother and replied, "Can you tell me what happened? If my son hurt yours, I will take care of it immediately." The other woman looked at her with surprise. That was not the reaction she was used to getting.

She immediately calmed down. She only wanted to be heard and acknowledged. G knew that. After all, she was a mother, too. They discussed what had happened. G spoke with her son, and they were all able to get things resolved. What could have turned into an explosive situation was averted due to the rational actions of an intelligent and confident woman.

One of the most popular of my seminars is "The ABC: The Anti-Bullying Campaign." As part of that program, I wrote a story called "The Dumb Fly." Would you like to hear it? (Of course you would.)

> The Venus flytrap, with its oval-shaped buds resting high atop long, fragile-looking stems, appears to be as common a houseplant as an African violet.
>
> However, beneath its fuzzy exterior lies a treacherous and deadly lesson.

Enter: an ordinary, black housefly with iridescent, transparent wings

and eyes atop its head that rotate 360 degrees.

Begin: "vegetative manipulation."

The Venus flytrap opens its buds and begins teasing the fly. Jagged edges, resembling teeth, should be enough to warn the fly of the dangers within. The plant continues its harassing. The fly moves closer. The bud widens, jagged teeth still proclaiming the perils ahead. But the temptation is too great. The fly cannot resist. He stupidly falls into the trap. Jaws immediately slam shut, and Venus begins to devour the prey.

"Ha! Another sucker! They never learn. Flies are so dumb!"

And another fly loses ... again.

How easily we fall into the traps of aggressors or bullies. They tease, torment, and intimidate us until we finally give into the temptation. We fall into their traps of retaliation and end up getting caught ourselves. Just like the dumb fly that gives in and ultimately suffers the painful consequences of its own stupidity, so do we sometimes fall into the same traps and suffer as well.

So, the question is: "Are you smarter than a dumb fly?"

Check one: yes _X_ no _____

(I checked yes for you. I know you are way smarter than the fly!)

Surely, there is someone in your life who presents challenges for you. Is it your boss, your spouse, a difficult neighbor, an aggressive driver? Whoever it is, decide to change the way you interact with them.

Develop a new strategy, a new course of action. Vow to do things differently. Then watch what happens. You'll need to decide for yourself what changes you are willing to make in order to produce a different outcome. Think it through carefully. Use your head.

Lock your ego in the closet before you begin. Think about the possible consequences of your choices. Consider all of your options. Choose the one with the best possible results *for all parties*, *now* and *in the future*. You can do it. I have faith in you.

DUCKS, DISHTOWELS, AND BIRTHDAY CAKES

I'd like to share with you two simple exercises you can practice that will definitely help you manage your anger much more effectively. Actually, one will help you to let go of a lot of it almost instantly. Imagine that! When an incident arises that you would normally get upset about, you will be able just to let go of it. You will automatically find yourself much more relaxed and in control of your emotions. The experience will require much less effort on your part to handle. And the great thing about this is that it's so simple to do.

This is an exercise I actually use with young children

when I work with them in schools. It's called the Great Duck and Dishtowel Debate. You'll need several props to do this exercise: a medium-size bowl, enough water to fill it, a small dishtowel, and a little yellow rubber duck (you know, like the one Ernie sings about on Sesame Street? "Rubber ducky, you're the one…"). This is how it works:

Fill the bowl with the water.
Place the dishtowel in the bowl.
Place the rubber duck in as well.
Pour some water over both.
Watch what happens.

The dishtowel will absorb the water, and the weight of the liquid will pull it down to the bottom of the bowl. The rubber duck, on the other hand, lets the water just roll off its back and manages to stay afloat.

In this incident, the water represents the negative experience you are having: someone said something cruel, you were treated unfairly by a family member, you were laid off from your job. Whatever it is, you have two choices about how to handle it and how to allow it to impact your life.

The first choice is to become like the dishcloth and absorb and retain the experience. You can personalize it and hold onto it. Negative experiences are weighty and can pull one down in life. They rob us of energy, enthusiasm, and joy. One can literally drown in anger, bitterness, resentment, etc.

Or, you can choose to be like a duck and just let it roll off your back. Someone insults you, and you can choose to let it go. It is what it is. You don't have to make it yours and carry it around with you for the rest of your life. You experienced it and choose not to hold on to it. That attitude keeps your spirits high and lends lightheartedness to the event. You stay afloat. Repeat after me:

It is what it is.

(Highlight. Let this be your new mantra.)

It's that simple. Refocus your thoughts. Put everything into proper perspective. Don't make a mountain out of a molehill. With everything in life that is really important, where does this rank? In ten years, will you even remember what happened? Probably not, so why make more out of it now than what it needs to be?

The more energy (thought/word) you give it, the more power it has. Don't relinquish your power to an event. Maintain control over your own happiness and destiny. Ask yourself: do I want to be angry, or do I want to be happy? The choice is yours. Remember, it's not about the experience. It's about what you choose to do with it. Life is only ten percent of what happens … remember?

The next exercise I'd like you to practice is called the Big Birthday Blowout.

Do you remember years ago, the best suggestion we were given for *controlling* our anger was to stop and count to ten? Did it ever work for you? Me neither. I can count to ten really fast, even faster if I count by twos. All this really did was delay the explosion. Definitely not the best technique.

The Big Birthday Blowout, however, is much more effective and certainly much more creative. This is how it works:

When you feel yourself getting angry, stop for a moment (kind of like the stop, walk, and talk technique you learned earlier).

Next, I want you to imagine that it is your birthday. (Congratulations, by the way. Sorry I missed it. My calendar broke again.)

Then, imagine your birthday cake, whatever kind you'd like to have. How big is it? What shape? Is it chocolate, vanilla, banana? (Banana? Yuck!) What flavor is the icing? Does it have strawberry filling, or lemon, or none at all? Does it have those big, sugary roses on top? Is your name written in gooey gel? (Mine would be a yellow sheet cake with mocha icing and lots of those roses—they're my favorite! And white filling, like the stuff in Twinkies, and maybe some sprinkles on the side would make it perfect. Yum! This exercise is making me hungry.)

Anyhow, I want you to go into great detail with this cake. And, you need to put candles on it as well. As many candles as you are in years, that's how many have to be on your cake. And no cheating!

Next, I want you to take a deep breath, and while slowly exhaling, sing to yourself "Happy birthday to me, happy birthday to me. Happy birthday, wonderful me, happy birthday to me!" Exhale and blow out your candles (in your mind, of course, so others can't see you. Otherwise you'll look totally foolish.) Repeat this process for each of the candles on your cake.

Are you crazy… again? Do you have any idea how old I am and how long this will take? Exactly. That's the point. Give yourself time to calm down. The deep breathing is a natural method to induce

JANET PFEIFFER

relaxation and relieve anxiety. The length of time this involves will allow you to rethink and reexamine your feelings and choice of behavior, hopefully avoiding any negative consequences.

And as an added benefit, if there is another party involved, she may get really bored waiting for you to work through this entire process and just walk away. Worst-case scenario: all of this deep breathing may cause you to hyperventilate, and you'll just pass out on the floor. By the time you come to, you won't even remember what happened. Problem solved. (*Just kidding* on that last one. You know me: always a comedienne. Gotta keep 'em laughin'!)

When I first developed this exercise, I was working with a group of children at the shelter. They were between the ages of seven and twelve. They were really angry kids and typically lashed out in violent and inappropriate ways. Needing something that would be fun and engaging while accomplishing my objective, I created this activity. And it worked.

One nine-year-old boy who had a quick temper came to me one day as proud as could be. "Janet," he said, "You know that thing you told us to do when we get angry, the one with the birthday cake? Well, I did it today at school, and it worked! My teacher said I did good."

He was so proud of himself. He didn't get into trouble the way he usually did. He found something that put him in control. He made a smart choice and felt powerful. Several years later, he told me he was getting along much better with his classmates. He wasn't fighting as much. When I asked him if he still used the birthday-cake exercise, he said not exactly. He told me he only needed to take some deep breaths, and he got the same results. He's not the only one who's proud of him.

THE FINAL
FRONTIER

We have certainly covered a lot of ground since the beginning of this book.

Hopefully by now, you have a much deeper understanding of what anger is and how to manage and express it more effectively. Equally, if not more importantly, I hope that you have also learned how not to get angry in the first place. In many instances, it's just not worth it. So much of what has angered us in the past, we now know is insignificant in the grand scheme of things.

However, I know there are still instances when the anger will surface. Even with the understanding and skills I have provided for you to use, we all occasionally have a lapse in memory or good judgment. Even I, "*The Great and Powerful Odd*"! (Get it? Like *Oz*, only I'm not... Oz. I am a bit odd though, don't you think? All right, *a lot* odd.) As much as I hate to admit it, from time to time I, too, find myself agitated and sometimes even irate. I can apply the principles I've taught you knowing that they will work extremely well.

But have you found, as I have, that although you have processed the anger and released it, there seems to be a tiny amount that lingers, that no matter how proficient you have become, there are those microscopic fragments that hold on for dear life? No matter how hard you try, you just can't seem to rid yourself of them and restore yourself to your desired state of serenity. Let me share with you the final stage of healing the anger.

It is called forgiveness. You've all heard of it. But how many of you have a clear understanding of just what forgiveness is? Plain and simple, I define forgiveness as *a conscious decision to let go of all residual anger that remains in the heart.* It is a choice to be at peace, to put the event to rest once and for all. Too many carry around inside them the pain from their pasts. They hold on to the emotions of prior experiences and keep reliving them.

You need not forget in order to forgive. In fact, I don't recommend forgetting. It is important to remember the event and to learn from it so you will not repeat it, but you don't need to keep feeling the pain.

Have you ever had a serious injury? Years later, you can still recall the exact event that occurred. However, if the wound has healed, you no longer feel the pain. So it is with forgiveness, only on a spiritual and emotional level. Remember the event, but don't revive the hurt.

Forgiveness takes into account human imperfections. It allows us to be human and make mistakes. That is not to say we do not need to be held accountable for what we have done. Of course we do. And we need to make sure we don't keep repeating those things. But we don't need to be held hostage either. There is a difference.

I can choose to be understanding and even compassionate of human imperfection. We are all struggling to get through life. It's not easy for any of us. I need to to refrain from judging others and encourage them to do better. I can be patient and pray for them to come to terms with whatever issues they are struggling with.

People act out what they are dealing with internally, remember? It is not humanly possible to get through life without ever hurting or offending others. And while I can try really hard to be a thoughtful and considerate person, at some point in my life, I have failed. So have you. So has each and every one of us. In his book *There is a Spiritual Solution to Every Problem*, Dr. Wayne Dyer says:

> Whenever you feel that someone has injured you or sullied your reputation or caused you physical harm, the spiritual solution, as difficult as it may appear, is to extend forgiveness. To hold onto the pain and seek to exact revenge will simply keep you stuck in pain and the problem will be exacerbated.

I encourage to you to heed his words. They contain great wisdom. If I want to be forgiven for my indiscretions, I must first be willing to forgive others for the times they have offended me. Remember what Gandhi said,

I must first be the change I want to see in the world.

(This is powerful. Definitely highlight.)

No human relationship can survive long-term without for-giveness. It is one of the key components to long, lasting friendships, business partnerships, and intimate relation-ships. And it is absolutely critical to creating global peace. But that peace must first originate within one's self. And it is not contingent upon whether or not the other confesses to any wrongdoing or even acknowledges it. This is something I do purely for myself. It is in essence a gift of self-love. I care enough about my personal well-being to restore inner tran-quility. Forgiveness is the key to inner peace. Remember,

We cannot be a world at peace until we are first a people of peace.

(Highlight this—make it your life's focus.)

SAY GOODNIGHT, GRACIE!

A message from my heart to yours: I want to thank you so much for taking the time to read this book. It has been fifteen years in the making. We live in a world filled with anger and violence. We cannot and *must* not continue hurting and destroying one another. I am determined to change that.

My mission in life is to bring a greater awareness of truth to those who are angry and hurting, to put an end to the senseless fighting and suffering we cause our families, friends, and ourselves. We can learn to live in harmony with others, but we must first create that peace within ourselves.

It's what we all want. Most of us just don't know how to do it. That's why I've written this book: to share my years of personal and professional experience of overcoming and healing the anger; to teach others how they, too, can create happiness, peace, and harmony in their lives.

You and I together can make a profound difference in bringing hope and healing to this angry planet. You and I together can begin to heal this world. But we must do it now. Time is running out.

I hope you have gained valuable insight from this book and trust that you will apply what you have learned in your daily life. You and those around you will truly benefit.

In the words of St. Francis, "Lord, make me an instrument of your peace..."

God bless you, my friend.

Janet

CONTACT INFO

Janet Pfeiffer
Pfeiffer Power Seminars, LLC
P.O. Box 2773
Oak Ridge, N.J. 07438
www.PfeifferPowerSeminars.com
www.FromGodWithLove.net
Janet@PfeifferPowerSeminars.com